THE WAY PEOPLE PRAY

THE WAY
PEOPLE PRAY

An Introduction to the
History of Religions

by

JOHN T. CATOIR

PAULIST PRESS

New York   Paramus, N.J.   Toronto

ACKNOWLEDGMENTS

Material from "Laotse, the Book of Tao" and "The Emotional and Artistic Life of Confucius" are taken from *The Wisdom of China and India*, edited by Lin Yutang, copyright ©1942 and renewed 1970 by Random House, Inc.; reprinted by permission of the publisher. Excerpts from the *Rig Veda*, translated by Manmutha Dutt, and from the *Talmud*, as translated by Lewis Browne, are taken from *The World's Great Scriptures*, © 1946 by Lewis Browne, and reprinted by permission of The Macmillan Co. The poems entitled "The Neanderthal Man Loved Flowers" and "A Liturgy" are reprinted by permission of their author, Catherine de Vinck.

Library of Congress
Catalog Card Number: 73-91369

ISBN 0-8091-1805-X

Published by Paulist Press
Editorial Office: 1865 Broadway, N.Y., N.Y. 10023
Business Office: 400 Sette Drive, Paramus, N.J. 07652

Printed and bound in the
United States of America

CONTENTS

This book is dedicated to my mother, may she rest in peace, and my father.

I am most grateful to Mrs. Lillian Lashendock, my secretary; Mrs. Emma Rosewall, my typist; and Mr. Gerald Costello, my editor, for their invaluable assistance in the remote and proximate preparation of this manuscript. A special word of thanks is also due Alleluia Press, Allendale, New Jersey, for granting me the privilege of using the extraordinary poetry of Catherine de Vinck.

1
GOD SPEAKS TO MAN

The Golden Rule, "Do unto others as you would have them do to you," is perhaps the most familiar and most basic ethical principle of mankind. Down through the ages, the human heart has been open to the whispering of exalted aspirations. In spite of the competition for survival, the tyranny of sexuality, the will to power and the violence which has resulted from the dominance of man's lower instincts, the human heart continually rises to sublime ideals. The dissonance and diversity of human experience seems to have one harmonious center from which emanates a power greater than the sum of the obstacles placed in the way of ultimate perfection.

The Golden Rule appears in many religions, differently worded but essentially the same in meaning:

Christianity:
All things whatsoever you would that man should do to you, do you so to them: for this is the law and the prophets. (Matthew 7, 12)

Brahmanism:
This is the sum of duty: do naught unto others which would cause you pain if done to you. (*Mahabharata* 5, 1517)

Buddhism:
Hurt not others in ways that you yourself would find hurtful. (*Udana-Varga* 5, 18)

Confucianism:
Is there one maxim which ought to be acted upon throughout one's whole life? Surely it is the maxim of

loving-kindness: Do not unto others what you would not have them do unto you. (*Analects* 15, 23)

Islam:
No one of you is a believer until he desires for his brother that which he desires for himself. (*Sunnah*)

Judaism:
What is hateful to you, do not to your fellowman. That is the entire Law; all the rest is commentary. (*Talmud*, Shabbat 3id)

Taoism:
Regard your neighbor's gain as your own gain, and your neighbor's loss as your own loss. (*Tai Shang Kan Ying P'ien*)

Zoroastrianism:
That nature alone is good which refrains from doing unto another whatsoever is not good for itself. (*Dadisten-i-dinik*, 94, 5)

The development of modern civilization from primitive antiquity has been a gradual climb toward that perfection. Prayer has many definitions but essentially it is prayer which has accounted for man's communication with the sublime. By moving away from the noise and confusion of life, man has found within his being a deeper life, a more satisfying level of existence which beckons him to go beyond his immediate sense experience. The voice of God is silent and still, speaking with irresistible sweetness to those who listen.

How can we trace the history of this voice, this spirit? We learn about the past from the present. Our parents reflect the characteristics of their great-grandparents, and they in turn reflect their ancestors. Recorded history only dates back about 5,000 years; before that we have only fossils, buried bones and ancient ruins to inform us of man's beginning. Man-like creatures roamed the earth more than two million years ago; the Darwinian hypothesis that man and the modern ape have a common ancestor ties us in some mysterious way to the early primates—whose development took some seventy million years. This vast historical spectrum staggers the imagination. In spite of the relatively strong appearance of an atheistic influence in the last one hundred years, there is overpowering evidence to suggest that man is a believing creature, in touch with his creator; he knows that his destiny exceeds the fleeting few years of his temporal life.

Prayer made man civilized.

Pray, for all men need the aid of the gods. (Homer, *Odyssey*, c. 800 B.C.)

Prayer is the greatest of spells, the best healing of all spells. . . . Amongst all remedies this one is the healing one that heals with the Holy Word. (*Yasht, Zend-Avesta*, c. 700 B.C.)

Prayer smites down the strength of all the creatures of Ahriman [the Zoroastrian "devil"]. It is the greatest, the best of all spells. (*Zend-Avesta*, 6th century B.C.)

He who offends against heaven has none to whom he can pray. (Confucius, *Analects*, c. 5th century B.C.)

An Angel collects all the prayers offered in the synagogues, weaves them into garlands, and puts them on God's head. (Meir, *Exod., R.*, 21, 4, *Zohar, Gen.*, c. 150 A.D.)

If apostles and martyrs, while still in the body, can pray for others, when they ought still to be anxious for themselves, how much more must they do so after they have their crowns and victories and triumphs? (St. Jerome, *Attack on Vigilantius*, c. 396)

He prays in the temple of God who prays in the peace of the Church, in the unity of Christ's body; which body of Christ consists of the many in the whole world who believe. (St. Augustine, *Ennaration on Psalm CXXX*, c. 415)

And why pierceth it heaven, this little short prayer of one syllable (God)? For it is prayer with a full spirit, in the height and breadth of his spirit that prayeth it. (*The Cloud of Unknowing*, 14th century)

Accursed the life of him in this world who breatheth without uttering the Name. (Guru Nanak, 1496-1538, *The Sikh Religion*, M. A. Macauliffe)

Granting that we are always in the presence of God, yet it seems to me that those who pray are in his presence in a very different sense; for they, as it were, see that he is looking upon them. (St. Teresa of Avila, *Autobiography*, 1565)

Prayer is always possible for everyone, rich and poor, noble and simple, strong and weak, healthy and suffering, righteous and sinful. Great is the power of prayer: most of all does it bring the Spirit of God and easiest of all it is to exercise. (St. Seraphim of Sarov, 1759-1833, *Conversation with Nicholas Motovilov*)

The shorter our allotted time is, the easier it perhaps is to decide to pray for one's enemies. (Soren Kierkegaard, 1813-1855, *Meditations From*, ed. T. H. Vroxall)

Be not forgetful of prayer. Every time you pray, if your prayer is sincere, there will be new feeling and new meaning in it, which will give you fresh courage, and you will understand that prayer is an education. (Feodor Dostoevski, *The Brothers Karamazov*, 1880)

What a spectacle for heaven and earth is not the Church in prayer! For centuries without interruption, from midnight to midnight, is repeated on earth the divine psalmody of the inspired canticles; there is no hour of the day that is not hallowed by its special liturgy. (Pope Pius XI, *Caritate Christi Compulsi*, 1932)

George Bernard Shaw, the Irish poet and playwright, once said, "Common people do not pray; they only beg." And perhaps this has been the greater part of the story of man's communication with the divine, the fact that he has so often, so frequently, been a beggar before his God. All the rituals and incantations of antiquity are related to this begging which is not only a plea for survival, but a search for meaning.

There has been a longing on the part of man and a corresponding response from God. In certain areas, such as the Golden Rule, a common understanding has emerged, a fundamental unity underlying the diversity of human experience. The longing that rises in the hearts of men everywhere, in every age, is basically a longing for security, total security, the desire for a love that endures, a happiness that will never tarnish. Survival here and now is certainly man's most immediate preoccupation, but he craves for something beyond his finite boundaries.

The "good life," *la dolce vita* of the West, does not bring the desired contentment; neither does the regulated life of the socialist state. Health benefits may be available to all, order may be insured by rigid law enforcement, but there is more to happiness than material security. An inner yearning for something beyond is at the heart of man's religious experience; man's sense of incompleteness causes him to cry out in anguish. Prayer is as natural to man as speech; it is the manifestation of his deepest longing, and his most exalted appeal to reality.

Man must also contend with misery. He is forced to coexist with sickness, failure, cruelty and pain. To make sense out of these experiences, not the least of which is death, he must explain them in some way. How can he harmonize the negative elements of existence with his inner longing for greatness, immortality, unending happiness? These are questions that man has been asking since the beginning. The Book of Job in the Jewish bible reminds us of this human yearning.

I am brought to nothing; as a wind thou hast taken away my desire: and my prosperity hath passed away like a cloud.

And now my soul fadeth within myself, and the days of affliction possess me.

In the night my bone is pierced with sorrows; and they that feed upon me do not sleep.

With the multitude of them my garment is consumed, and they have girded me about, as with the collar of my coat.

I am compared to dirt, and am likened to embers and ashes.

I cry to thee, and thou hearest me not: I stand up, and thou dost not regard me.

Thou art changed to be cruel toward me, and in the hardness of thy hand thou art against me.

Thou hast lifted me up, and set me as it were upon the wind, and thou hast mightily dashed me.

I know that thou wilt deliver me to death, where a house is appointed for everyone that liveth.

But yet thou stretchest not forth thy hand to their consumption: and if they shall fall down thou wilt save.

I wept heretofore for him that was afflicted, and my soul had compassion for the poor.

I expected good things, and evils are come upon me: I waited for light, and darkness broke out.

My inner parts have boiled without any rest, the days of affliction have prevented me.

I went mourning without indignation; I rose up, and cried in the crowd.

I was the brother of dragons, and companion of ostriches.

My skin is become black upon me, and my bones are dried up with heat.

My harp is turned to mourning, and my organ into the voice of those that weep.

Our purpose is to study the history of man's religious heritage, not merely to quote beautiful passages from the sacred writings of the world's great religions, but to consider them in context.

The way a man prays is greatly influenced by the way he views the world, the way he lives his life. His understanding of his surroundings has always influenced the way his longing for the beyond would find its expression.

When men were hunting or fishing for survival, animals played an exaggerated role in their spirit-life. They saw in the beasts a life beyond the visible; conversely, higher beings were often envisioned as animals.

There is a legend passed on from generation to generation among the U.S. West Coast Haida Indians. A long time ago, a bear lived in the woods. He was enormous and fierce. When hunger drove him, he would come out and ravage their ancestors' camp. Many were killed, and the braves determined to destroy the beast. They tried everything they knew to lure and trap him, but he always eluded them, outwitted them and by some mysterious intelligence escaped unharmed. For years he survived their best efforts and eventually they came to believe the bear was endowed with a superior spirit. Their fear slowly turned to admiration which, in turn, led them to make peace with their enemy. Incantations to his spirit were sung in the night and ritual dances were designed to imitate his movements in a hymn of praise.

The name "animism" is defined as the belief that nature, and animals in particular, possess individual souls which may exist apart from their material bodies.

When you understand this background, the hymns and rituals of the Haida become charged with a new meaning. Even though we do not share that same limited world-view, we can appreciate the human heart behind these primitive manifestations of worship.

In later centuries when man tilled the soil for his livelihood, other natural objects took on greater significance. The sun, the wind, and the rain, for instance, were personified as divine powers. As we have seen, the emphasis on the worship of nature did not necessarily preclude an understanding of some supreme power.

Generally throughout history man's prayer has expressed the same basic longing, the same desire to befriend the superior powers and achieve lasting happiness. Out of this human need a multiplicity of religious traditions and rituals have evolved. The field of study has become so complicated that a separate science has emerged, the science of comparative religions.

The present book is an introduction to the religions of the world—with particular emphasis on the importance of prayer in man's religious experience. Each one of us can grow to appreciate his own faith or belief in God by examining the heart of his fellow man in the act of believing, of reaching out beyond the narrow confines of individual life.

We learn from exposition, but also by contrast. What do other men seek in life? What was ancient man like? Did he worship God? Did he believe in an afterlife? Do primitive religions have any similarities with the faith of modern man? What about the ancient religions of the East: Hinduism, Buddhism, Confucianism, Taoism? How do these systems of belief resemble Christianity? How do they differ? What relationship does prehistoric religion have to Judaism? Who was Mohammed, and how did he, a preacher who never performed a miracle, achieve such amazing success in the spreading of his faith? In what way does Islam relate to the Black Muslim movement in the United States?

Important questions in the study of comparative religions are: How do all these religions fit together? How do they relate to one another? How do we make sense out of them all? Three approaches are possible, but remember that an approach to the question is not necessarily the answer. An approach refers merely to the point of view held by the reader as he begins to assimilate the mass of religious material before him.

(1) You may choose to study comparative religions with a predetermined intent to establish your own faith as preeminent by proving that little significant truth can be found in other religions. This view seems truncated and foolish when one believes in a good and loving God who in his own way must have manifested something of himself to the millions of men who sought him in past ages.

(2) You may maintain that all religions are basically the same, since they all more or less denounce selfishness and promote the Golden Rule. But we know there are significant differences between the major religions, and we cannot pretend that they do not exist. The common elements of man's religious history do not obscure the obvious discrepancies. All religious sects stress their own special understanding of the truth; in many cases their conclusions are incompatible. Some will say that Christ was divine; others, that he was merely a great moral teacher, an itinerant rabbi, nothing but a man. These ideas are believed by serious religious-minded people. We cannot say that an idea is correct merely because the believers are sincere. All religions are really and objectively different.

(3) You may seek to experience other faiths by listening to their teachers and learning from those who have sought the living God down through the ages. In this approach, you do not close your mind to the striking beauty of truth when it manifests itself in other faiths, nor do you find all religions saying the same

thing. You see not only the rich variety of beliefs, but
also the mysterious unity underlying the apparent differences. In other words, you grow in understanding.

The major religions of the world may tend to urge
men to have love for one another by following the
Golden Rule, but love implies acceptance, and acceptance, understanding, so that men cannot truly rise to
love unless, and until, they strive to understand one
another.

As a prelude to this understanding, we must keep
in mind a point made earlier. The language, culture and
political structure of every human society is profoundly
influenced by the particular way in which the people interpret the world in which they live. Every person is a
unique composite of many traditions. People do not fit
neatly into predetermined slots. Yet it is important for
our purposes to distinguish the categories of thought
which have evolved in history.

I. *The monist world-view.* Here, emphasis is
placed on the principle of unity underlying the entire
universe. God, man, nature and the spirit-world are all
seen as elements of one undivided whole. Each visible
thing, living or nonliving, animal, vegetable or mineral,
is seen as a superficial manifestation of a single invisible world-soul. This all-pervading world-soul is called
"Brahman" by the Hindus. The Hindu law of Karma,
which is the basis of the belief in reincarnation, states
that everything which now exists emanated from one
unit of primeval matter and will be absorbed into it at
the end. The word "absorbed" is important here because it implies that individuality is snuffed out at
death. Consequently, for many Asians, individuality
exists only in the present life, and the "now" counts for
very little.

II. *The polytheistic world-view.* Polytheists generally pay no heed to any sense of solidarity in creation. They are preoccupied with each and every power which has supernatural dimensions. The nature-worshipers, the animists, the worshipers of mythical gods, all participate in polytheistic religion. These people generally live in awe and fear of the spirit-world. They identify many natural events with divine beings and give them names: there is then a god of thunder, a god of rain, etc. Yet the world-view of ancient man is too complex to be summarized under the simple heading of polytheism, since we cannot exclude the influence of the monist view among primitives. The monist view sees God, man and nature as one being; polytheism sees man and nature as distinct, while attributing god-like qualities to natural objects; monotheism sees man and nature as distinct, while believing in only one supreme God.

III. *The monotheistic world-view.* Believers in one God can be divided into two categories: the theocratic and the incarnational. A theocratic world-view sees God as a personal creator, absolute, individual and totally other, not as the impersonal, abstract unifying force of the monists (pantheists). Here the supreme godhead exercises full authority over all creation and favors some creatures over others according to his pleasure. The dominant Father-figure, characteristic of the God of Judaism, is an example of this view. An infinite chasm separates creatures from their creator; God is personal, but totally apart from his creation. Christianity differs in that it is incarnational.

The incarnational world-view has grown out of the theocratic: God has come down to "dwell among us," so that the separation between man and God is bridged. This view differs also from monism, in that each being

is seen here as distinct, individual and radically different from any other, including God. Yet, in the incarnational view, God, man and nature are seen to com-
municate much more fully. For Christians this entire
disjointed universe is reorganized within the being of
the Messiah, Jesus Christ. Man and nature are mysteri-
ously reconciled and totally immersed in God. The immanence of God in the created universe explains the at-
traction Christians have for the monism of Eastern
religions. Both immanence and monism more or less
emphasize the divine presence here and now, in all
created reality, but each in its own distinctive way.

IV. *The atheistic world-view.* Agnostics and militant atheists see man as supreme in the universe; he can
master nature and solve all problems through science
and technology. Man, in the last analysis, is his own
savior. Agnostics and militant atheists know of no
other answer to the riddle of human pain and sorrow.
They see no way out beyond death and total extinction.
They seek the absolute of freedom within the chaos of
absurdity.

It is within the context of these four views that
human history has developed and is developing.

The way a man prays will be determined by the
view he has of himself and of the world in which he
lives. Even the atheist is said to pray in the foxholes of
mortal combat.

QUESTIONS TO THINK ABOUT

1. How can you account for the presence of the "Gold-
en Rule" in so many religions of the world?

2. Nearly every religious faith, Christianity included, claims to be a movement to unify mankind. Why, then, do these beliefs often divide people from each other?

3. Through all the ages, religious beliefs have led people to engage in an activity called prayer. Why do people pray? Why is it that you do or do not pray?

4. Do you believe there is an instinct deep within one's being that does not come from learning or tradition? Is there such a thing as "natural religion"?

2
PREHISTORIC RELIGION

If we compare Mother Earth to a woman one hundred years old, she would have lived in loneliness—without the company of humans—for over ninety-nine years, eleven months and twelve days. She would have lived with human beings a little more than eighteen days, and with civilized man no more than twenty minutes!

The earth is over four billion years old. The first truly manlike species appeared about two million years ago. Fish preceded man by nearly four hundred million years, reptiles by two hundred and seventy-five million, dinosaurs by one hundred million. Manlike creatures, not yet human, predated him by more than seventy million years. Civilized man, that unique intelligent species which now dominates the planet, is a newcomer among the living.

How We Know about Prehistoric Times

Through their explorations and diggings, archeologists have learned much about our ancestors from their tools, pottery, carvings and ruins. Such findings serve as clues to prehistoric man, to his way of life and scale of values. Yet, in the absence of recorded history, this information can only be speculative. The first written records appear about 5000 B.C.—which means that for tens of thousands of years before Abraham (1850 B.C.)

human societies existed of which we know almost nothing.

How, then, can we understand primitive man's religion? By deduction. Sherlock Holmes would say, "Elementary, my dear Watson!" Every historian knows that present facts are the consequence of what has gone before, so that existing cultures provide clues about the past which sometimes reveal a complete way of life. Religious historians often begin by studying the mythologies and cultures of primitive people still living at the present time: the Pygmies of Zaire or the Aborigines of Australia. By comparing the beliefs, practices and artifacts of such people with the ancient remnants discovered by archeologists, they are able to discern elements common to both recent and remote cultures. No absolutely accurate conclusion may be drawn, but such comparisons give rise to working hypotheses leading to a deeper understanding of mankind's solidarity.

We know, for instance, that primitive man was as concerned as we are with death and the afterlife; elaborate burial rituals demonstrate this dramatically. Food, weapons and the equivalent of money were often buried with the deceased to help him in his new life. Yet, it is useless to try to discover a totally pure and original form of religion; pure religion never existed. No religion can be reduced to any one form or structure, although common elements are found in many widely separated cults. Certain forms may predominate in certain societies, but never exclusively; different rites, myths and symbols coexist in every religion. That is why it may be misleading to offer precise examples of primitive practices taken out of context, since the emphasis of a tiny part of a tradition might distort the true image of primitive man.

Even with the data of archeology, we know little about primitive man. We know that he hunted, ate, feared, loved and died as we do. An appealing expression of this link we have with our primitive ancestors is found in a poem by Catherine de Vinck, called "The Neanderthal Man Liked Flowers":

Words and silences
break into many parts:
            fragments of life, mosaics
not yet completed
                        the gaps open like wounds.

The wind comes out of the North,
alive with leaf-sounds . . .
            Did it, in the beginning, blow dust
at the mouth of the cave, curl
            the smoke of the first fire?
The moon, three-quarter full,
                        and silver-drunk,
            slides through chinks in the clouds.
What word was used to speak of the moon?
What small tactile hands built
                        a clumsy altar
to honor the god moving distantly
                        in the sky?

Long unexplained pauses cut up
the story of man: time spaces
            through which he filtered
to new skills, new shapes, new naming,
            pressed by obscure need
from one stratum to the next,
from one ledge of precarious being
                        to another,
            across what gulf, what line of tension,
            holding
                what tenuous thread?

Scars on a hillside, old campfires
            with magic circles of stones, tombs
            deep in the rock, a people
                        passing
            in the far distance, lost and reborn,
gathering flowers for the dead.

Ancient man had crude theologies and moral systems with severe taboos. Most prehistoric societies also had liturgies related to hunting, fertility and puberty. Initiation ceremonies and burial rituals were undoubtedly common to all tribes.

These common features found in man's religious history from prehistoric to present times cannot be explained merely by the handing down of customs year after year. There have been tribes and civilizations entirely cut off from the world, isolated from others for centuries by oceans and impassable mountain ranges, and yet their religious beliefs and customs are very similar to those of others halfway around the world, with whom they could not possibly have had any contact. Something within man himself seems to produce a constant pattern of religious practices.

The Emergence of Polytheism

Long after Neanderthal man (c. 180,000 B.C.), primitive men struggled in intellectual darkness. The forces of nature (tornados, floods, earthquakes, scorching sun) were frightening to him either in their own right or as forces animated by some mysterious being. He experienced the forces of nature as personal events, either for the good or for the destruction of his tribe. Since he had no satisfactory explanation of recurring natural calamities, he always felt threatened by unseen powers lurking behind visible reality.

He took steps to make peace with these ominous beings. There was no way he could control the forces themselves, so he called upon his own powers of persuasion to induce these superior beings, as he thought of them, to treat him kindly. Early man was in constant communication with the spirit-world through his mental defensive system expressed through rituals and incantations.

Most atheists trace man's earliest religious instincts to this combined sense of fear and wonder, a condition, they assert, stemming from his own ignorance. But they forget that primitive man had a questioning mind. Man has always known that what exists could not have come from nothing. Throughout the ages, people have asked: "Why am I here? Where am I going?"

If early man was obviously polytheistic, preoccupied with many gods, it does not mean that he was totally ignorant. There is an abundance of evidence to demonstrate that primitive men all over the world carried in their legends and oral traditions a rich heritage of human values and even signs of a knowledge, or distant memory, of one supreme God. After they had exhausted all the avenues of recourse to the minor deities, the God of gods was there to hear them.

The Supreme Being apparently lessened in importance precisely because of his great superiority. The ordinary affairs of men were too far beneath him. Most anthropologists today conclude that polytheistic systems are not what they seem. Our primitive ancestors were very much like us. The veneration of the saints today is a barely disguised form of the early reverential instinct. We find Catholics praying to St. Anthony when they have lost their keys or their wallets because the God on high is too important to be pestered with trivial matters. Hindus, Muslims, Buddhists and Taoists have similar provisions for these petty concerns.

Ancient men were not that unusual in their prac-

tice of naturism. "When the help of all other gods and
goddesses has proved disappointing, the Oraon turn to
their Supreme Being, Dharmesh: 'We have tried everything, but we still have thee for our helper'" (Mircea
Eliade, *Myths, Dreams and Mysteries*, p. 136). The
presence of mythologies with a multiplicity of superior
beings does not lead to the denial of an instinctive
awareness of one Supreme Being. On the contrary, it
seems to support it. This opinion is shared by most
religious historians today.

Most of the polytheistic systems had a network of
minor deities; a person could call on the god or gods
who had jurisdiction over his problem. There was a god
for each village, a god for the mountain nearby, a god
for the wind and the river; in fact, everything seemed to
be animated by the spirits, even the animals. Animism
is the name given to this form of primitive worship.

Each spirit had to be propitiated in a special way.
Man had to cope with unknown powers and forces, and
he created mysterious rituals for that purpose. For instance, even today in primitive societies, hunters, after
killing their larger prey, will disembowel the animal
and crawl inside its body to establish good relations
with its spirit, so that the spirit will not depart the beast
and do harm to the hunter later.

Rites of Initiation

Initiation rites are common to nearly all religions,
and our primitive ancestors had elaborate rituals, pain-
fully and meticulously detailed, to achieve a specific
purpose. The rites of initiation into puberty are classic
examples: they always involve a symbolic death fol-

lowed by a symbolic resurrection. The revelation of tribal doctrinal secrets to the candidate constitutes the new life, the new experience of the sacred which will characterize his or her admission to adult circles.

Perhaps you saw the movie *Walkabout* where a young Australian aborigine begins the first phase of the ritual. In nearly all initiation rites the mystery begins with a separation from family and tribe, a retreat into the desert or forest. The death symbol is implicit, for the desert or woods represent the "life beyond." The candidate must survive on his own, overcoming personal fear and alien powers. In the movie, the young native comes upon a lost teenage white Australian girl and her six-year-old brother abandoned in the desert. The lost girl and her brother had traveled for a few days, barely surviving, when across the desert came the lean, black aborigine with spear in hand and a half dozen lizards hanging on his belt. His face was painted with bright characteristic markings. The plot unfolds as the three become friends, and in spite of language and culture differences, the city girl and her brother are guided back to safety. It is a picture of rare quality.

Our interest is in the Australian aborigine. He is on his "walkabout," on his trial in the wilderness, preparing for initiation into the adult male assembly of his tribe. In most tribes throughout the world, there is an initiation hut, tepee, or cave set aside in the bush or the desert. Here the young man receives instruction concerning the tribal secrets. The hut symbolizes a womb. The candidate must stay in the fetal state for a determined period of time. His emergence is a symbolic birth, "the dawn of the first day," as the Australian Karadjeri call it.

Some tribes then cover the boy with white powder,

in the likeness of a ghost; he must behave as a returned spirit in his ritual dances, gestures and incantations. He is then tortured and mutilated and scarred by the elders to prove he endured the ordeal. His mythical ancestors have symbolically devoured his spirit; it is as though he were digested in the belly of the initiatory monster. Later, a specific ritual operation takes place; in the case of the young male, it is circumcision. A new name is given and the previous life is over. Circumcision is not a Jewish invention, as so often believed.

After the walkabout, the tribe anoints the young Karadjeri from head to foot with human blood. Later, his nose is pierced and a quill is passed through the wound. Circumcision does not take place until about two years later, and then the young man is called *Miangu*, which signifies that he is at an advanced stage of the initiation process. Another ceremony follows, called the *Laribuga*, where the initiate climbs a tree while the men of the tribe sing a sacred song. Usually a climbing rite signifies an entry into the world above, a symbolic ascension into heaven. Many other Australian myths and rituals among the primitive contain these ascension ceremonies.

Still the initiate is not finished. A number of intermediary ceremonies follow until after several years the *Midede* ceremony takes place. The young man then is led by an old man to a secret place where they bury the primal, or ritual poles. The myth of the Bagadjimbiri is then revealed through song and dance. It is their creation myth, a story of two brothers who came up out of the earth in the form of dingos, or wild dogs, which gradually grew to become two human giants. Before the Bagadjimbiri nothing existed at all, neither animal, vegetable nor human and even the ceremony of the buried

primals, and the dance itself is said to have been invent-
ed by the Bagadjimbiri. The secret of the tribe's origin
is revealed.

A missionary once produced a ballpoint pen in
New Guinea and the natives examined it closely, returned it and asked, "Who made it?" A simple question, but very revealing of their simple curiosity. Who
could explain the manufacturing process that produces
a pen? The native merely wants to know who made it,
and he wants to know who made him.

The initiate's passage from adolescence to manhood, once completed, constitutes the boy's full formal
indoctrination into the secrets of the tribe and serves as
his formal education, his religious instruction, and his
diploma. He learns about his origins, he knows how he
came to exist. Nearly all the tribal rituals of the Karadjeri are said to be directly designed by the founding
Bagadjimbiri. This creation myth, like countless others,
is one example of man's fundamental need to come to
terms with his origins. In nearly all creation myths
something comes into being from nothing. Something
or someone who always was, and who did not need to
be created was responsible for the origins of man. The
rich variety myths from every corner of the world are
all designed to express this intuition.

The Fear of the Unknown

Remember, the Karadjeri are a primitive tribe living today in Australia. We conclude from evidence
found through archeology that primitive men who existed long before recorded history were doing many of the
same basic things.

The ancient burial rituals discovered through archeological diggings correspond in many details with the practices of contemporary primitives. We begin to have a feeling for our ancient ancestors, we begin to understand a little, the kind of being he was and how much we have in common with him. Yet we have only scratched the surface. It is very easy for modern man to misread the symbols and come to conclusions which are not accurate; much more must be learned to fill the blanks in our knowledge.

Even today in primitive tribes there are practices which appear to be something other than what they are. The contemporary New Zealand aborigine is careful to bury his hair, nail clippings and waste materials. One would think this springs from a desire for cleanliness, but it does not. He is afraid that some hostile person or spirit might come into possession of something that was part of his own body and that enemy would automatically have power to do him physical harm.

The voodoo doll of Haiti is based on a similar principle. By doing harm to a replica of a person, that person is struck by the evil spell. All kinds of incantations and counterattacks are designed to protect against such a travesty. The prayers and music of witches, shamans or medicine men, are designed to allay such fears, many of which still persist in modern men.

There can be little doubt that our primitive ancestors were crippled with superstitious fears. They treated outsiders as enemies. Their world was a hostile, frightful place.

A good example of this might be found in certain African rituals of exorcism. In the Lango district in North Uganda, an area between five and six thousand square miles, many tribes coexist though the Lango tribe is the largest, numbering in the neighborhood of a quarter million. The Lango are a Nilotic people, long-limbed, black, lean and muscular. They worship ancestral spirits as well as the one high god they call Jok. No one has ever seen him, and they think of him as the winds. When many deaths occur at once because of disease or pestilence, they attribute it to the path of Jok. Like the air he is omnipresent. He is the creator of sky and earth and he is generally thought of as benevolent, though given to occasional fits of jealousy. He punishes very severely if he is not properly worshiped.

In his capacity as protector of souls he is called Jok Orongo. The idea of Jok in the mind of the Lango includes the sum total of the long-departed merged into one pre-existing deity (Jok), a plurality of spirits unified in the person of a single godhead, a spiritual force composed of innumerable spirits, any of which may be temporarily detached without diminishing the oneness of the force. This includes the souls of certain animals, like giraffes, rhinoceroses, elephants. For some reason lions and leopards are not thought of as possessing souls.

This concept is slightly different from the Hindu idea of Brahman where all spirits, indeed all reality is merged into Brahman, thus losing all individuating characteristics. In Jok, a ghost here and there can spring loose. Sometimes a ghost will come back to haunt or annoy his family or his former enemies. A shrine is then built to pacify him. Once in a while a ghost will not be satisfied and will continue to harass the tribe, so it becomes necessary to put him or her to rest once and for all. At this point they summon a medicine man (the *ajoka*, which simply means a man of Jok). He comes and ceremoniously kills a he-goat and smears the blood on the stomach and chest of the person or persons who are haunted by the ghost. He shakes a rattle during this procedure to protect himself, and prepares a small new-made jar with a narrow mouth for the catch. In the jar is placed some food which the deceased ghost is supposed to have liked in his lifetime. The jar is a trap baited to attract the ghost. He calls the ghost by name to come and take his food. The ghost of course is suspicious and begins to ask questions. The *ajoka* tells the ghost he is among friends, all of whom are assembled to watch the expected capture. If any are absent the reason for the absence is explained to the ghost to reassure him. Once secure that everything is up and up the ghost, who *now* believes he is invited to a family feast, enters the jar to eat the food his soul loves so much.

At once the *ajoka* slams a lid on the jar and fastens it tightly. The jar is carried away and buried in the middle of a swamp. As time passes the stray spirit is once again absorbed into Jok where he belongs, and he no longer threatens the tribe. Sometimes a captured ghost will scream out and threaten to kill them all if they do not let him go. Out of fear they may actually release him provided he promises to be content with his shrine and leave them in peace. If he agrees they take off the lid, and place the jar near his shrine to remind him that he can expect punishment if he is tempted to annoy or harm them in the future. According to Sir James Krager, "It is to the credit of ghosts in general that no such case of a backsliding ghost is on record."

The Power of the Word

Even today these dark shadows of fear cross the

minds of modern men who should know better. If we are more conscious, more sensitive to the dignity of man today, it is because of increased enlightenment. Through the ages we have developed and changed. Our understanding of natural events and our awareness of the proper dimensions of the spiritual have delivered us from many fears which haunted our ancestors. But we must not forget that much of the pseudosophistication of contemporary man is a deliberate inadvertence to the mystery which surrounds his very existence and destiny, the mystery of life, death and afterlife.

Rollo May in his book *Love and Will* raises the question, "How does one know that among the bedlam of voices which beset us all, one is really hearing his daimon?" Whether a man goes to his soothsayer, his priest, his psychiatrist, or his counsellor, he is still searching for answers to his fears, and to the apparent powers that threaten his life. In each instance there are words spoken to him, words which give him an understanding of what is happening to him. Dr. May says that naming the daimon, personalizing the impersonal, has been and still is the traditional way man overcomes the daimonic. Jesus calls out "Beelzebub!" or "Legion." Exorcists who are successful are able to divine the name of the evil spirit. Today in psychotherapy the therapist seems to succeed in relaxing his patient when he names the evil power which holds him. You have an inferiority complex, or you have extrovert tendencies coupled with repressed hostility toward your mother, or you hate your doctor because of transference, a disguised and suppressed hatred of your father. Words seem to give the patient the sense of penetrating the mystery of his own life, of having received something for his money. "This relief does seem to have the characteristic of the 'magic' of words," says Rollo May.

There is a power in the word, a power given to man, communicated originally in the form of symbols and myths; with this power he enters combat with evil and sickness of soul. Christians believe the word is made flesh and is still dwelling among us. The power of the word is total, giving man supremacy over the dai-monic forces in himself and in the world around him. Man is still in need of protection for survival. We cannot laugh at our ancestors and their primitive dances, for we are all men, and we are all in need of light and truth and the word.

QUESTIONS TO THINK ABOUT

1. Were the religions of primitive people silly? Would they have been happier without any religion? Explain.

2. Would you consider modern Christians, Muslims, or Jews more religious than primitive peoples? Why or why not?

3. What superstitions still persist in your family? Do you, personally, have any superstitious practices? Where did they come from?

4. Assuming there truly is an all-powerful God, isn't it natural to fear him? Or should religion seek to eliminate the fear of God?

3
EGYPTIAN CIVILIZATION

The ancient Greeks were young when Egypt was a declining empire. The Greek historian, Herodotus, writing five centuries before Christ, said that Egypt contained "wonders more numerous than those of any other land, and accomplishments so great as to be beyond description." Primitive men were still nestled in caves and huts all over Africa, Asia and parts of Europe, when this ancient civilization began to blossom along the banks of the Nile River; it was a culture which grew in richness and splendor, enduring as an empire for more than 2500 years. This unparalleled stability of an entire civilization is in itself one of the great marvels of world history.

The History of Egypt

The earliest Egyptians came to the Nile Valley from somewhere else, we do not know where. They were like the English and French coming to the shores of America, dislodging the primitive inhabitants. It is believed by Egyptologists that 6000 or 7000 years ago these invaders entered from the South, probably from what is today called Somaliland, Africa. Attracted by the Nile's fertile valley, the nomads came and settled, building the marvelous civilization of ancient Egypt.

Villages sprang up rapidly. The surrounding desert discouraged foreign invaders, and a peaceful society de-

veloped. The villagers learned to trade with nearby
towns, cooperating rather than warring with one another. Eventually they merged and organized themselves to control the Nile's annual flood for mutual protection, so all could benefit from the rich mud deposits
left behind when the water receded. Organization on
the political level soon followed, and the inherent gift
for governing became manifest in the leaders who
emerged. Ultimately it was the gift of wisdom in government which explains Egypt's amazing longevity as a
state.

By 3500 B.C. the villages had formed two major
political entities: the Kingdom of Upper Egypt and the
Kingdom of Lower Egypt. Since the Nile flows from
south to north, and the earliest settlers entered from the
south, the south was called Upper Egypt; Lower Egypt
was in the north, toward the Mediterranean Sea.
Around 300 B.C. the great King Menes of Upper Egypt
conquered the north, i.e., the delta region of Lower
Egypt, and for the first time the two Kingdoms were
united under one rule: the Kingdom of Upper and
Lower Egypt.

It was the world's first real nation under a single
monarch, the Pharaoh of Egypt. This succession of
pharaohs continued for 30 dynasties. The first two dynasties alone covered almost 400 years. Then the history
of the Nile people is divided into three periods: the Old
Kingdom, the Middle Kingdom and the New Kingdom.
An Egyptian historian named Manetho recorded this
dynastic history around 3000 B.C., at a time when
Egyptian civilization was slowly waning.

The Old Kingdom lasted from 2700 B.C. to 2200
B.C., the period when the pyramids were built; the
Middle Kingdom from 2000 B.C. to 1800 B.C., the

period of greatest economic expansion; the New Kingdom lasted from 1600 B.C. to 1100 B.C. After 1100 B.C. Egypt began its decline, though pharaohs ruled the nation up until the 4th century B.C.

The pharaoh was the supreme ruler in Egypt. All power was in his hands. He was not only a king, but gradually he became a god. By the 5th dynasty the pharaoh was not just a god but the incarnate son of Re, the supreme Sun God. As divine monarch, he lived in lush splendor, holding massive power over the lives of millions; it was not difficult for peasants to imagine him as a descendant of Re. The pharaoh was worshiped in temples throughout Egypt and revered everywhere in the kingdom.

It was logical that when a god returned to the afterlife, he deserved a fitting tomb. The pharaohs of the Old Kingdom built the most imposing edifices known to man: the pyramids. In the early period they were buried not only with food, money and jewelry to keep them happy in the next life, but also with the bodies of their servants who were ceremoniously sacrificed to accompany them on their voyage to Re. This practice of human sacrifice was abandoned before the end of the Old Kingdom by a more merciful succession of pharaohs.

Strange as it may seem, Napoleon Bonaparte played an important role in developing the science of Egyptology. In 1798 he travelled there with an army of 38,000 men in 328 ships to conquer the Nile and cut off England's direct route to India. His ambitions to conquer Europe depended on striking a fatal blow to the British economy. But his motives were also scientific. He was fascinated by a newly awakened interest in Egyptian culture which was flourishing on the continent

at that time, and he organized a team of scholars, bota-
nists, naturalists, historians, linguists and artists to join
in the expedition and study Egyptian civilization in de-
tail. About 200 of them were hidden among the soldiers
when Napoleon landed on July 2, 1798.

The Turks who then occupied Egyptian territory
gave his army very little trouble in their invasion. Soon
the French dictator set his scholars to work amassing a
vast treasury of historical data, pictures and artifacts.
The British were not standing idly by; they knew Napoleon's grand ambition, so a British fleet under Admiral
Nelson slipped into the harbor at Abukir and totally
destroyed the French ships. Napoleon was stranded
with his army in the hot unfamiliar desert terrain. They
had been trapped for many months when Bonaparte
decided to sneak out with a hand-picked group of his
scientists. He secured a ship, and slipped through the
British blockade, abandoning his army in October of
1799. By 1801 the British and Turks had destroyed the
poor French soldiers left behind, but Napoleon had returned safely to Paris where he published the results of
his findings in a 36-volume work entitled, "Description
of Egypt." The military expedition was a disaster, but
the scientific discoveries were an enormous success,
providing stimulation and information to archeologists
and researchers for decades to come.

The Faith Experience of the Egyptians

Religion was so deeply ingrained in Egyptian life
that human survival was thought to depend on it. There
was no separation of religion, economics and government as we know it today. Religion was central to all

human activity. The political framework itself was a theocracy.

Primitive Egyptians were no different from other primitive people. They had a great respect for the wonders and mysteries of nature. Animals were held in awe for their varied abilities and traits. Ferocity in the lion, strength in the elephant, faithfulness in the dog, were deified. The first set of Egyptian gods were characterized as animals. Prior to the pharaohs, polytheism was standard, animism was as natural to the Egyptian as the sun rising and setting. A spirit was seen as the cause of every natural event.

In the early stages of Egyptian life, the jackal, an animal which is known to dig up human bones, was the image given to Anubis, the god of the dead. Heavy stone vaults were common in graveyards precisely to protect the dead from the hungry jackal. Egyptian art depicts many of these and other magnificent animal gods but as time passed divine images became more refined.

Re, a local god, was first worshiped in Heliopolis, a Greek name meaning "The City of the Sun." Re, the God of the Sun, was the first god to achieve nationwide recognition. He reigned supreme for a long while, but he always had to compete with other minor deities.

Another well-known but lesser Egyptian god was Osiris, the ruler of the netherworld. Maybe he was a real ruler whose reputation reached legendary proportions, or a god of fertility, perhaps, left over from primitive worship, but he is believed to have created Egyptian civilization. His evil brother Seth was jealous of his prominence, so he slew Osiris. But the slain king was resurrected through the plodding perseverance of his wife, Isis, who searched for and collected his dismem-

bered body, piecing the bones together. Horus, their
son, avenged his father's death, slaying Seth and gain-
ing the right to rule Egypt. It was believed thereafter
that every pharaoh ruled as Horus, and when he died,
he became Osiris. The new pharaoh then took over to
rule on earth as Horus once again, renewing the cycle.

The system of Egyptian deities tends to overlap.
There are many gods, many ideas of creation and also
many different views of the afterlife. The Re cult, or
solar cult, believed that the dead pharaoh simply board-
ed the sun's heavenly boat to sail across the sky each
day. It may be interesting to review the concept which
ancient Egyptians had of the universe. The world was
envisioned somewhat as a cube. The earth provided the
floor, and the mountains on the edges of the floor held
up the sky. The cube was suspended in space and another sky was underneath the earth. The sun was
thought to go under the earth and around it at night.
The cult of Osiris did not believe their pharaoh sailed
with the sun. When he died they imagined he passed
into the netherworld or underside of the earth to rule
below as he once ruled on earth.

In the beginning of the Old Kingdom, the quality
of immortality was attributed only to the pharaoh and
his family. By the end of this period nobles were included, and they were allowed to have their tombs close to
the pharaoh's tombs. It was a kind of sharing immortality by association.

The changing social structure of Egypt in the Middle Kingdom allowed a more democratic approach to
heaven, and ordinary mortals were permitted to enjoy
the blessings of afterlife. Magic, rituals, liturgies and
sacred rites, once the exclusive property of the
pharaohs, became public property and the priestly caste

grew in importance. Burial ceremonies were the chief preoccupation of these people who were careful to prepare themselves for the next world. They believed that the afterlife involved a full human existence, not a mere spirit-life. The soul rejoined the body in heaven, and this belief is the basis for the Egyptian practice of mummifying their dead.

It was hoped that by preserving their bodies from decay they would enhance the process of resurrection, and provide themselves with a decent start in the new cycle of life. The dry climate was conducive to successful experimentation in the mummification of the dead, but the secrets of this ancient art are still a mystery to us today. The priests who performed it were thought of as acting in the role of Anubis, the god of the dead, who restored Osiris to life after Isis had collected his bones.

The pharaohs were entombed in the pyramids, but paupers were wrapped in a coarse fiber and buried in a communal cemetery. Even the poorest graves contained food and other articles which would help the deceased in the next life. There were literally millions of these graves all along the Nile Valley, but through the centuries most of them have been looted, including the great pyramids.

The religion of Egypt had an ethical character as well. It was believed that a sense of law and order, a quality called *Maat*, was built into the world by the gods; it was something like our concept of the natural law, but translated literally it means order, truth, justice or righteousness. For the Egyptian, *Maat* meant hard work and honest treatment of neighbor. After the decline of the Old Kingdom life became hard and *Maat* became identified with a sense of social justice, but in the Middle Kingdom prosperity eventually returned, and as life became easier, *Maat* was again seen as a law set down by the gods. That meant that any dissent about the structure of society or the power of the pharaohs was forbidden. Reform was unthinkable, revolution an impossibility. The gods had created the world; it was a static world. Everything was just the way the gods wanted it. Any dissenters who pitted themselves against the gods and the armies of the pharaoh were virtually committing suicide.

In this culture the act of creation was seen as one final piece. There was no Garden of Eden, no period of past glory, no future age which would be different or better. It was a static world, cut and dry, in more ways than one. The afterlife would be the same as this life but only the best of this life would be preserved.

The lifelong concern with death and the elaborate preparations for it were the major religious preoccupation of the Egyptian. Worship and moral propriety had their role, of course—one would not expect good treatment from the gods without it—but feathering one's nest, in a material sense, i.e., getting a well-prepared tomb, was a chief concern of Egyptian faith.

There was a decided evolution toward monotheism which reached its peak in the New Kingdom during the reign of Amenhotep IV (1375-1350 B.C.). The people were ordered to renounce all their gods and worship the one true god, Aton. By this time the priestly caste which tended all the shrines of all the gods had grown in power and prestige. Amenhotep struck a blow at their power by exalting Aton as the One God in the universe, the master of life, the creator of all that is. All other gods and their shrines were nullified with one stroke. One of Amenhotep's Hymns to Aton is our earliest record of monotheistic worship.

> The dawning is beautiful in the bottom of the sky,
> O living Aton, Beginning of Life!
> When thou risest in the eastern horizon
> Thou fillest every land with thy beauty,
> Thou art beautiful, great, glittering,
> high above every land.
> Thy rays, they encompass the lands, even
> all that thou hast made.
> Thou art Re, and thou carriest them all away captive
> Thou bindest them by the love.
> Though thou art far away, thy rays are upon earth;
> Though thou art on high, thy footprints are the sky.
>
> Thy rising is beautiful, O living Aton, Lord of Eternity;
> Thou art shining, beautiful, strong;
> Thy love is great and mighty,
> Thy rays are cast into every face.
> Thy glowing hue brings life to hearts,
> When thou hast filled the Two Lands with thy love,
> O God who himself fashioned himself,
> Maker of every land,
> Creator of that which is upon it:
> Men, all cattle large and small,
> All trees that grow in the soil,
> They live when thou dawnest for them.
> Thou art the mother and the father of all that
> thou hast made.
> As for their eyes, when thou dawnest,
> They see by the means of thee.
> Thy rays illuminate the whole earth.
> And every heart rejoices because of seeing thee,
> When thou dawnest as their lord.

The richness of monotheism dominated Egypt for a while but the deeply imbedded polytheistic practices continued to live, a strong devotion to the many other gods still held power over the imaginations of the people. It was Amenhotep IV who, by insisting on the worship of one supreme God, paved the way for the worship of Allah in what is now a Muslim Egypt.

Religious Practices of the Egyptians

Egypt was monotheistic. Egypt was polytheistic. It was never exactly one or the other. The supreme god was the one god, but the many gods of legend and myth endured in the minds and memories of Egyptians for generations. No matter what gods a particular priest served in the Middle Kingdom, he had specific rituals to observe. Every morning, for instance, from one end of the Nile Valley to the other, a standard ritual was practiced for centuries. After rising a group of priests would take a ceremonial bath in their sacred pool. They would clothe themselves in vestments and enter the temple in procession. The public could watch the priests enter the temple courtyard but were not permitted to enter themselves. Inside the temple the chief priest would wait for the first rays of the morning sun and then he would open the sanctuary doors revealing the effigy of the lord god, a mummy-like figure smaller than a man. All priests prostrated themselves and chanted prayers of worship, while the air was clouded with incense to purify the area for the god's appearance. The chief priest would take down the statue, change its garments, perfume it, and set it back in place as the sun rose slowly in approval. Food and drink were provided before the sanctuary doors were closed and sealed with clay until the next morning when the same ceremony was repeated.

There were periodic festivals when the routine was adjusted to allow the common folk a gaze at the effigy. The festival procession through the village where peasants lined the streets to watch was considered not only a privilege given to the people, but also a day of entertainment for the god. One particular celebration took place in Abydos, the site of the early pharaohs' tombs. Osiris' head is supposed to have been buried there. Throughout Egypt a pilgrimage to Abydos was carried out once a year and those who could afford it made the journey. At this festival the Osiris resurrection myth was reenacted.

The average Egyptian celebrated his own future resurrection. Whereas formerly only the pharaoh was guaranteed immortality, by the Middle Kingdom the ordinary man who was considered a son of pharaoh became worthy of immortality. The following inscription is taken from "Coffin Texts," (I, 197 and translated by R. T. Rundle Clark in *Myth and Symbol in Ancient Egypt*, London, 1960, p. 134). It gives the sense of the common man's self-image in ancient Egypt.

> Now are you a king's son, a prince,
> As long as your soul exists,
> so long will your heart be with you.
> Anubis is mindful of you in Busiris,
> your soul rejoices in Abydos where your
> body is happy on the High Hill.
>
> Your embalmer rejoices in every place.
> Ah, truly, you are the chosen one!
> You are made whole in this your dignity
> which is before me.
> Anubis' heart is happy over the work of his hands
> and the heart of the Lord of the Divine Hall is
> thrilled when he beholds this good god.
> Master of those that have been and Ruler
> over those that are to come.

The priests were always present to implement the beliefs of their people. In those days the priest shaved all his hair, including eyebrows and lashes; he lived a life of monastic purity and dressed in a white loincloth to set him apart from all other members of society. Those in full-time service were the only ones allowed to enter the innermost sanctuary of the temple. Others of lower rank were specialists of one kind or another: scholars, musicians, singers or scribes. The latter would leave their occupations to live in the temple one month out of four. Women also served as part-time priestesses, but most of these served as singers and musicians.

The preparation of others for the afterlife was a major duty for the priests. If the deceased was rich, the burial rite might take as long as 70 days to complete. A poor man could be wrapped up in about a day and a half. Salts, spices and resins were mixed in a concoction and applied to the dead body in order to preserve it. It would then be swathed in layers of cloth, varying in quality according to the wealth of the family. When the preparations were complete the deceased was returned to the family for funeral services.

The usual prayers were read and one rather unusual event took place. It was an "opening of the mouth" ceremony which was performed as the last rite before entombment. The body was made ready in this way to eat, drink and converse with the gods in the next life. The procession, or parade, to the tomb which followed has been depicted on countless stone carvings of Egyptian tombs. Burial was always away from town toward the West where the sun begins its nightly journey under the world. The procession might travel for miles, across the Nile by barge, and on ox-driven carts to the burial site. Ritual chants were sung along the way by bareheaded priests who burned incense to purify the air. The procession would end at the door of the tomb and a final ceremonial dance would be performed as the chant continued. The following prayer is a final preparation for burial.

*None Returneth Again
That Is Gone Thither*

How prosperous is this good prince!
It is a goodly destiny, that the bodies diminish,
Passing away while others remain,
Since the time of the ancestors,
The gods who were aforetime,
Who rest in their pyramids,
Nobles and the glorious departed likewise,
Entombed in their pyramids.
Those who built their (tomb) temples,
Their place is no more.
Behold what is done therein.
I have heard the words of Imhotep and Hardedef,
(Words) greatly celebrated as their utterances.
Behold the places thereof;
Their walls are dismantled,
Their places are no more,
As if they had never been.

None cometh from thence
That he may tell (us) how they fare;
That he may tell (us) of their fortunes,
That he may content our heart,
Until we (too) depart
To the place whither they have gone.

Encourage thy heart to forget it,
Making it pleasant for thee to follow thy desire,
While thou livest.
Put myrrh upon thy head,
And garments on thee of fine linen,
Imbued with marvelous luxuries,
The genuine things of the gods.

Increase yet more thy delights,
And let (not) thy heart languish,
Follow thy desire and thy good,
Fashion thine affairs on earth
After the mandates of thine (own) heart.
(Till) that day of lamentation cometh to thee,
Then the silent-hearted hears not their lamentation,
Nor he that is in the tomb attends the mourning.

Celebrate the glad day,
Be not weary therein,
Lo, no man taketh his goods with him,
Yea, none returneth again that is gone thither.

The asceticism of the Egyptians revolved around death, and the longing in the human breast for meaning to life transcending this world. All the religions of the modern world express this same ancient longing.

QUESTIONS TO THINK ABOUT

1. Why have people looked upon their rulers as gods? Has this tendency totally disappeared in modern times?

2. What is the connection between believing in a god and believing in an afterlife? Is it possible to have one without the other?

3. How does the fact of death affect your own religious beliefs?

4
JUDAISM

The word "revelation" has profound meaning when contrasted with the ignorance and superstitious fear of primitive man. Many people think of ancient Judaism as the beginning of religious consciousness. The Adam and Eve story in the book of Genesis certainly reports our beginnings but when one considers it was written around 587 B.C., around the time of the Babylonian exile, it becomes clear that the Judaic-Christian story was written quite a few million years after the fact. Yet, like every creation myth it carries the same religious teaching. A supreme God created all that is out of nothing. There is a difference in the Adam and Eve story, and the key to this difference is in the phrase, "And he saw that it was good." Creation is good: flowing from a good God.

We can gain deeper insight into the beginnings of Judaism by looking more closely into the Babylonian civilization which flourished as far back as 3000 B.C., more than 1000 years before Abraham.

Around 1850 B.C., Abram was the leader of a nomad tribe originally somewhere in ancient Persia. Abram, as he was called, is the Father of the Jewish faith. His name was changed to Abraham by God. He had migrated to Palestine from an ancient culture which was basically polytheistic, from a people who believed in many fearsome gods. The significant thing about Abraham is his total surrender to Yahweh.

His Babylonian ancestors believed their own prevalent creation myth, that man was created out of the blood of a slain god. Their creation story was an attempt to put order into the incredible disorder of human life. Accordingly, Abraham's childhood beliefs about creation might very well have followed the ancient myths of his people, beliefs which mirrored the turbulence of their own lives. The rivalries and cunning of men were seen as a reflection of the power struggles found among the gods.

The chief Babylonian god was Apsu, who was married to Tiamat, a giant female dragon. Ancient Persia was a land of violent storms and flooding. All the floods were attributed to the activity of the gods Apsu and Tiamat. These gods had offspring, two of whom were Anu, the lord of the heavens, and Ea, who ruled over all the rainstorms. The son of Ea, who is called Marduk, eventually became the most important of the deities, because he prevented Tiamat and her illicit lover Kingu from destroying all the gods in an attempt to seize power. Marduk killed Kingu, and it was from Kingu's blood that man came into being. This is the Adam and Eve story of a major civilization which flourished around 3000 B.C.

The One God

Babylonians believed that man was the corrupt offspring of an illicit love affair between two power-hungry gods. To them the creator was not good and his offspring was not good. Life for the Babylonians was much like the myth, a struggle filled with bloodshed and violence. It was not difficult for them to explain the mysteries of the universe in these terms. Abraham no doubt was influenced by these myths which attempted to explain life. No wonder he was stunned by the new understanding of God that was revealed to him. He learned first that there was a supreme God; and he learned that God was a good God; a personal God, a loving Father. But the most dramatic personal fact for him to learn was that man himself was good and not a vile offspring of some minor deity. He had come from a world where man was a mere plaything for brutal and selfish gods who in their superhuman combat caused the natural disasters which ravished people's lives. This new understanding of God changed everything for him and for his people. A devotion to Yahweh developed that became the basic character of the Jewish people.

An evolutionary change from polytheistic to monotheistic faith took place with the life of one man, and his new vision affected countless people for generations down to the present day.

Abraham reacted against a former tradition. His followers gradually abandoned the Babylonian belief in man's essential corruption and his dependence on the whims of capricious gods. Abraham received a totally new vision of man's relationship with God. Yahweh had mercifully spared Isaac.

An important principle is demonstrated here, for as we shall see time and again, in the study of other religions, major changes in religious beliefs come about when great religious leaders reacted against the existing traditions of their day.

Around 500 B.C., Prince Gautama, who became the Buddha, the "Enlightened One," reacted against the interminable cycle of reincarnation and the fatalism of ancient Hinduism. He was a Hindu before he tried to start a new path to God which is now called Buddhism.

Around 620 A.D., Mohammed reacted against the chaos and polytheism of the Arabic world of his times, citing Allah as the one and only God.

Ancient Egypt was perhaps the first world civilization to move from polytheism to monotheism, calling the sun the one true god. Today, Egypt is almost entirely Muslim, following Islam, the religion of Mohammed.

Concerning the devotees of each religion, it is obvious that there is a vast difference between the spirit of the founder and the lives of his followers. The teachings of a master by no means guarantee that his followers do what he asks. For instance, Christ said, "Love your enemies," but Christians seem to have a great deal of trouble just trying to love their friends and relatives. When Mohammed asks a follower to give every year, two-and-a-half percent of his entire wealth to the poor, it does not mean that all Muslims obey. Giving away one-fortieth of all you possess is a considerable act of charity, especially if it is required year in and year out. When the Buddha says that selfish desires must be extinguished before one can truly be called enlightened, it does not follow that all Buddhists are selfless.

The noble intuitions of the founders of the great religions of the world are admirable in their own right, even apart from the degree to which they are integrated into the lives of the devotees of each respective religion. Very few people follow anything or anyone in exactly the same way. Therefore, it is impossible to analyze the nature of each major religious belief on the basis of data received from the current practices of its followers. There are as many Buddhist sects as there are Christian (Protestant, Catholic and Orthodox). All of them are of differing shades, all of them attempting to follow their master in a different manner. The complex process of action and reaction creates divisions and changes, sometimes small, sometimes great. Abraham's reaction to his own past was induced by a process which Jews, Christians and Muslims believe to have been initiated by God.

Judaism evolved in three stages. The first stage was under Abraham. As the leader of a nomad tribe he travelled from a land where, in addition to the major deities, each clan had its own god. Abraham's clan was no exception. It was Abraham's total conversion to Yahweh that is the basis of Jewish monotheism.

The second stage of Judaism did not come until 1285 B.C. when Moses established the covenant with Yahweh after the exodus. The Ten Commandments were given by God to Moses and Abraham's descendants became a religious nation, named after Israel. Abraham's grandson, Israel, had twelve sons; each was a father of one of the twelve tribes. It was Moses who inspired a sense of unity to the twelve tribes, and the sons of Israel became one nation.

The third stage of Jewish evolution took place in the activity prophets who spent their lives and lost their lives still trying to purge their people of the primitive, superstitious and idolatrous instincts which persisted from their Babylonian heritage. Monotheism was not universally practiced even among the followers of Yahweh. In this period the prophets made it more and more emphatic that Yahweh was not merely their national God but the one and only God, the God of Gods. The first commandment given to Moses stressed this belief: "I am the Lord thy God. I shall not have strange gods before me." This teaching was pounded into the Jewish nation by the prophets Isaias, Jeremias, Job, Joel, Jonas, etc., until no one could misunderstand its meaning: there is only One God; all other worship is idolatry.

Around 1000 B.C., Israel reached a high point in its development. When David conquered Jerusalem, Israel became a kingdom. King David was revered as the crowning blessing of God, and the prototype of the Messiah still to come. He was succeeded by King Solomon who built a temple in Jerusalem but the monarchy soon waned in the face of warring opposition from neighboring tribes.

It is a characteristic of new-formed states that the national god becomes a personification of the power of the state, the way Marduk was for the Babylonians, but Israel was different. The state did not make Yahweh; Yahweh made the state. When the monarchy began to decline, it was seen as Yahweh's punishment, for Yahweh made the kingdom and he alone could break it. The prophets had predicted the nation would dissolve because of its infidelity to Yahweh, and the prophecy proved true. First the kingdom split in half. Around 721 B.C. the northern half of the kingdom called Sarall, with its capital in Samaria, fell into the hands of the Assyrians, and in 587 B.C. the southern half, called Judah, with Jerusalem as its capital, fell to the Babylonians. Exile and destruction should have snuffed out every vestige of the Jewish faith, but instead there was a faithful remnant which carried on belief in Yahweh more tenaciously than ever. Most of those who returned after the exile were from Judah, the southern half of Israel, and the next 500 years of Jewish history are dominated by their slant on the meaning of their religion. Judaism was the name given to the tradition from this point forward.

Tragedy still plagued the Jews. First there was the occupation of their land by the Greeks and later in 63 B.C., they were invaded by the Romans. Jerusalem and the whole territory surrounding it was a captive of Rome. Judaism endured many persecutions down through the ages and has survived them all.

The Faith of a Jew

There are three elements basic to the Jewish faith: God, the Torah and the People. First, there is *God* who comes to man to arrange a covenant, a testament or an agreement with his chosen people. Then there is the *Torah*, the first five books of the Bible which constitute the law, but it is more than the law, it is the name given to the total "way of life" which God chooses for his people.

God teaches a *pattern of life* which he asks his people to embrace so that he may build them into a community made in his own image and likeness. The third element is the *People* themselves, a chosen race set apart from others to be formed by God through obedience to his spoken word. Here is the Covenant, the Old Testament. God chooses his people and says, "I will be your God and you will be my people if you accept my Commandments." The people did accept them, and in spite of sporadic infidelity to that commitment, an infidelity challenged over and over again by the prophets, the agreement was sealed.

Every Jew is a descendant of Abraham the father of the faith, but it was Moses who spoke the words which are repeated by devout Jews every morning and evening of their lives:

"Shema Yisroel Adonoi Elohenu, Adonoi, Echod (Hear, O Israel, the Lord our God, the Lord is One)." This prayer sharply distinguishes the Jewish faith from all forms of polytheism: God is one, supreme, personal, and interested in his people. Unlike the Hindus and Buddhists, life for the Jews is not an illusion to be overcome or a curse to escape from, but a gift of God, à kingdom prepared for his chosen people. Their rituals and prayers celebrate this approach toward God's gift of life.

But to be faithful to this good God, one must seek his holy Will. Life must always be lived according to his plan which is contained in the *Torah:* Genesis, Exodus, Leviticus, Numbers and Deuteronomy.

Over the centuries, the ancient laws and teachings of Moses were added to, modified, strengthened or slackened to suit contemporary circumstances. Most of these changes were part of an oral tradition passed along by the rabbis, generation after generation. It was not until six centuries after Christ that this body of tradition and commentary on the Torah was put into written form and called the *Talmud*. It was a compilation of sayings, metaphysical speculations, science, astronomy, history, and legends which became the source of religious inspiration for the many Jews scattered all over the world from Europe throughout the Near East. The temple was destroyed and the geographical center of the faith was replaced by this living book of sacred writings. The Diaspora is the name given to the scattered Jews, and the local synagogue became the center of each community's religious life.

Orthodox, Conservative and Reform

Fidelity to the law of the Torah, and the prescriptions of the Talmud is central to Jewish piety, but the approach taken to these obligations varies greatly among Jews. For instance, the Sabbath, the day put aside in the Torah for rest and the contemplation of God, is an important day for the Jewish family. The Sabbath has been described as a day on which there is presented a foretaste of the world to come. The day is celebrated with special food, songs, and pious practices.

Orthodox Jews follow the literal interpretation of the sacred books. No secular or mundane activity is allowed on the Sabbath, nor do they engage in any work or travel. They do not pick up the telephone, write letters, go shopping or even touch money on that day. When an Orthodox rabbi conducts services on the Sabbath, he will have to get someone who is not a strict Jew to turn on the lights of the synagogue, open the doors and lock up when everyone has left.

The Conservative Jews relax these strict observances. They remain true to the spirit of the law without feeling the need to go to the extreme of literal observance. Substantially the same ritual is followed, but exceptions are made when sufficient reason presents itself.

The Reform Jew usually ignores the prohibitions of the Sabbath. Many Jews call themselves Reform Jews because they have virtually abandoned all religious practices and yet they do not want to abandon their Jewishness.

There is a beautiful quality of praise of God in strict Jewish worship. Prayer practices which date back centuries before Christ include a strong emphasis on the concept of the praise and blessing of God. It can be presumed therefore that Jesus recited the same traditional prayer patterns of all good Jews. According to Robert Aron, author of *The Jewish Jesus:* "One must understand that in such a setting steeped in religion, the act of blessing is, for Jesus as for any Jew of his time, the key to his relationship to the universe. All events of daily life or natural phenomena are greeted with an appropriate blessing. And this network of blessings is, for each Jew and the whole of Israel, the basis of their participation in the life of the universe and in the unfolding of history."

The principle behind this worship is very simple. All of creation is seen within the sacredness of Yahweh. This sense of the sacred is reaffirmed throughout the life of a good Jew. In communal worship the blessing comes from the whole group. Jewish prayer is unlike Muslim devotion in that it is not an occasion for simultaneous individual private prayer. The whole Jewish community blesses and praises Almighty God with one voice.

God promised Abraham that he would be given the power to bless, a power which was proper to God alone. "I will bless you and make your name so famous that it will be used as a blessing" (Genesis 12:2). From Abraham the power was transmitted to the priests and prophets and eventually to all the people in their prayer rituals. Everything that is used and enjoyed by men is the occasion of a blessing. It is profane to use God's creation without uttering praise of God in the form of the blessing. The day is filled with opportunities for these prayers. In the morning the religious Jew prayed a blessing which was recited no doubt by Christ himself. "Blessed art thou, O Lord our God, King of the

Universe, who opened the eyes of the blind . . . who settest free them that are bound." The morning preparations of washing and dressing are accompanied by the prayer:

> Blessed art thou, O Lord our God, King of the Universe, who hast hallowed us by the commandments, and given us command concerning the washing of the hands.
> Blessed art thou, O Lord our God, King of the Universe, who clothest the naked.
> Blessed art thou, O Lord our God, King of the Universe, who bringest forth bread from the earth.
> . . . who createst various kinds of food.
> . . . who gives goodly scent to fruits.

It should not be difficult for the Catholic reader to recognize the prayer at the Offertory of the Mass, a prayer rooted in the Jewish tradition:

> Blessed are you Lord God of all Creation, through your goodness we have this bread to offer which earth has given and human hands have formed, it will become for us our spiritual food.
> Blessed are you Lord God of all Creation, through your goodness we have this wine to offer, fruit of the vine and work of human hands, it will become our spiritual drink.

The Jewish ritual is loaded with similar prayers for all occasions: when one receives good news or bad, when one meets a friend, on the occasion of trial or temptation. The most solemn blessing is the one uttered at the synagogue service by the officiating rabbi. The priestly blessing is seen as a blessing of God himself, and this is the solemn moment of the Jewish liturgy.

The Sabbath ritual begins at sundown on every Friday. The woman of the house is surrounded by her husband and children as she lights the Sabbath candles

with the blessing: "Blessed art thou, O Lord our God,
King of the Universe, who has sanctified us by thy laws
and commanded us to kindle the Sabbath light." The
father then blesses the wine and everyone takes a sip,
praising God for the wine which is praised as a "symbol
of joy." This ritual begins the twenty-four hour Sabbath period.

The Orthodox Jew will attend synagogue service
Friday evening after dinner, Saturday morning for the
main liturgy, and again Saturday afternoon. There are
almost as many Orthodox Jews as there are Conservative and Reform Jews put together; so while a greater
openness and flexibility is present in Jewish worship,
the predominant body of the faithful adhere to the
strict observance.

The Friday evening service has begun for centuries
with the song of the Sabbath, Psalm 92:

> It is good to give thanks to Yahweh
>   to play in honour of Your Name, Most High,
>   to proclaim your love at daybreak
>   and your faithfulness all through the night
>   to the music of zither and lyre,
>   to the rippling of the harp.
>
> I am happy, Yahweh, at what you have done;
>   at your achievements I joyfully exclaim:
>   "Great are your achievements, Yahweh,
>   immensely deep your thoughts!"
>   Stupid men are not aware of this,
>   fools can never appreciate it.
>
> The wicked may sprout as thick as weeds
>   and every evildoer flourish
>   but only to be everlastingly destroyed,
>   whereas you are supreme for ever.
>   See how your enemies perish,
>   how all evil men are routed.
>
> You raise my horn as if I were a wild ox,
>   you pour fresh oil on my head;

I was able to see those who were spying on me,
so the virtuous flourish like palm trees
and grow as tall as the cedars of Lebanon.

Planted in the house of Yahweh,
they will flourish in the courts of our God,
still bearing fruit in old age,
still remaining fresh and green,
to proclaim that the Lord is righteous,
my rock in whom no fault is to be found!

This is followed by the *Barekhu*, the blessing which is still the solemn moment of the service. The leader says: "Bless ye the Lord, who is blessed . . ." and the congregation responds, standing and slightly bowed in the direction of the table on which the scrolls of the Law are laid, saying in one voice:

"Blessed be the Lord, who is to be blessed forever and ever."

The most important religious days are Rosh Hashanah, Yom Kippur and the Passover. Rosh Hashanah is a two-day holiday celebrated at the start of the Jewish New Year when the shophar is blown. Yom Kippur is the Day of Atonement, a fast day celebrated on the tenth day of the month of Tishri. Passover is an annual feast which was instituted to commemorate the passing over, or sparing of the Hebrews in Egypt when God smote the first-born of the Egyptians.

The first Passover is described in the Book of Exodus:

And the Lord spoke unto Moses and Aaron [Moses' brother] in the land of Egypt, saying: ". . . And they shall take of the blood [of the lamb], and put it on the two side posts and on the lintel, upon the houses wherein they shall eat the flesh . . . with bitter herbs they shall eat it . . . and yet shall eat in haste—it is the Lord's passover.
For I will go through the land of Egypt in that night,

and will smite all the first-born in the land of Egypt.
. . . I will pass over you . . . and this day shall be
unto you for a memorial, and ye shall keep it a feast to
the Lord . . . for ever."

The Passover liturgy begins with the *Seder* meal. It
was this meal which became the Last Supper of Jesus
on the night before his passion and death. The meal itself is an ordinary dinner, with some special foods. The
ritual that accompanies the meal is distinctive, however, and the sacredness of the occasion is stressed in its
commemorative dimension. It begins with a dialogue
when the youngest child asks, "Why is this night different from all other nights?" The father replies, "We
were slaves unto Pharaoh in Egypt and the Eternal,
Our God, led us from there with a mighty hand."

The prayers and food requirements are all speci-
fied in the Sacred Scriptures. The *matzoh*, of course, is
unleavened bread which is called the "bread of affliction." It was unleavened bread which was taken in
haste during the flight from Egypt. *Haroset* is a paste
made from apples and nuts and it is remembered as
food used by the Jews while they performed slave-labor
for the Pharaohs.

Jews of strict observance still believe that the Messiah will one day come, and a glass of wine is put out at
the Seder meal for the Prophet Elijah who will announce his coming at a Passover meal.

One of the important readings during Passover
week is the memorable passage from the Prophet Eze-
kiel:

The hand of Yahweh was laid on me, and he carried
me away by the spirit of Yahweh and set me down in the
middle of a valley, a valley full of bones. He made me

walk up and down among them. There were vast quantities of these bones on the ground the whole length of the valley; and they were quite dried up. He said to me, "Son of man, can these bones live?" I said, "You know, Lord Yahweh." He said, "Prophesy over these bones. Say, 'Dry bones, hear the word of Yahweh.' The Lord Yahweh says this to these bones, 'I am now going to make the breath enter you, and you will live and you will learn that I am Yahweh.' "

I prophesied as I had been ordered. While I was prophesying, there was a noise, a sound of clattering; and the bones joined together. I looked, and saw that they were covered with sinews, flesh was growing on them and skin was covering them, but there was no breath in them. He said to me, "Prophesy to the breath; prophesy, son of man. Say to the breath, 'The Lord Yahweh says this; come from the four winds, breath; breathe on these dead; let them live!' " I prophesied as he had ordered me, and the breath entered them; they came to life again and stood up on their feet, a great, an immense army.

Then he said, "Son of man, these bones are the whole House of Israel. They keep saying, 'Our bones are dried up, our hope has gone; we are as good as dead.' So prophesy, say to them, 'The Lord Yahweh says this; I am now going to open your graves; I mean to raise you from your graves, my people, and lead you back to the soil of Israel. And you will know that I am Yahweh, when I open your graves and raise you from your graves, my people. And I shall put my spirit in you, and you will live; and I shall resettle you on your own soil; and you will know that I, Yahweh, have said and done this—it is the Lord Yahweh who speaks.' " (Ezk. 37: 1-14)

When God's will is fulfilled for his people he will bind together the dead, the fragmented, the disoriented people of Israel and breathe into them a new life, new level of being. The promise of a messiah to restore the kingdom is a promise still enduring in the hearts and minds of many of the sons of Israel. Among Christians it is believed that the messiah has already appeared in the person of Jesus Christ.

QUESTIONS TO THINK ABOUT

1. Can you think of any reasons to explain the apparent historical development from polytheism to monotheism? Does monotheism "work better"? Is it more sophisticated? Explain.

2. Devotion to Yahweh was the most powerful force in the unification of the Hebrew people. Do all religions play similar roles in the creation of group identities? Give examples.

3. What possible value can be found in religious laws such as fasting or prohibitions from work on certain days?

4. "All of creation is seen within the sacredness of Yahweh." How does this knowledge affect the life of the pious Jew? How do *you* regard creation?

5
CHRISTIANITY

We are all familiar with the Christmas story: the child in the manger, the young mother Mary and her husband, Joseph, seeking shelter in a stable where they were warmed by the breath of beasts; the three wise men who followed a brilliant unusual star and offered the child gold, frankincense and myrrh.

The word "epiphany" is used to commemorate the event of the wise men coming to the child; it means a showing forth, an unveiling. But what the gospel depicted is the revelation, not of a powerful king surrounded by a splendid court, nor of any such symbol of power which the world might recognize and respect, but what is shown is a child, a weak, helpless infant in his mother's arms. Christians are asked to look upon this infant, to believe he is the son of God, the very image of God's splendor, the face of his love; to recognize him as the lord of history, the messiah, the savior, the truth, the way, the life.

To the Christian the wisdom of God contradicts the wisdom of the world and can well be called folly. As St. Paul says, "The foolishness of God is wiser than men and the weakness of God is stronger than men."

The Mystery of the Incarnation

There are many Christian denominations with differing creeds, but they all share a faith in Jesus Christ, the Son of God who came in the person of an infant, born in a small country during a time of oppression. Indeed, it does seem a mysterious folly, one for which there can be no logical explanation, and one for which no one can offer any scientific verification. The happening cannot be categorized or classified, it defies analysis and the laws of logic, yet the world is asked to accept the reality of God crying with an infant's cry, eating, sleeping, growing up and dying a man's death.

The world is asked to accept the manifestation of love, not in abstract terms, but in the reality of body and blood, in the full presence of a man in "our image and likeness," one who can weep, suffer, bleed and die. This is the mystery that is shown to the world in the revelation of Jesus Christ, and Christians believe it with awe, love and joy. The child in Mary's arms is the Lord, the Son of God, the one who holds the keys of the kingdom. The message of his coming tells us over and again that the Father loves us with a love so reckless that he gave mankind not a formula, a philosophy, a symbol to show the way of reconciliation, but he gave his very own son in the person of Jesus Christ.

This is the mystery of the incarnation.

Christians celebrate and proclaim their faith in this revelation, they accept his lordship over their lives. They imitate the wise men and offer him their gifts, their faith, their gratitude, and their praise for all they have received from his hands. They bring him their joys and sorrows, the lifted chalice of their lives, the gold, incense and myrrh of all their days. They see the world as charged with his splendor, and they understand that their own poor weak and mortal selves are changed and forever blessed with the power of life in him, and through him, and with him, Jesus Christ the messiah.

Glory to God in the Highest, and on earth peace to men
of good will. (Lk. 2:13)

Roman Catholics, the Eastern Orthodox, Quakers,
Lutherans and all others who call themselves Christians, believe in the incarnation, each with their own interpretation.

Cardinal Newman, the most famous convert to
Catholicism in the 19th century, in his "Essays on the
Development of Doctrine," stated that the doctrine of
the incarnation was the leading idea of Christianity.
His thesis has become the foundation of the present
Constitution of the Roman Catholic Church, a thesis
which was formulated and codified at the Second Vatican Council (*Lumen Gentium*). According to Cardinal
Newman, the incarnation has three aspects: the sacra-
mental, the hierarchical and the ascetical. Every idea in
the Church can be reduced to one of these three categories united within the central concept of the incarnation. God became man, the word was made flesh. In
this mystery Christians believe Christ intends to make
his followers into what he is himself, a person united to
God the Father for all eternity. This is what it means to
rise in Christ.

Jesus' disciples believed that he was God. They
were convinced of his love for them and for all mankind. "Greater love than this no man hath, than to lay
down his life for his friend." The love of God was no
longer a divine attribute, or an abstract idea—it was
the person of Jesus Christ. The power of God's love for
man was realized most dramatically in the example of
Jesus.

Christ's divinity is still a stumbling block, as it was
even in the beginning. Not until the year 325 A.D., during the Council of Nicea, did the Fathers of the Church

face the question of whether Christ was of the same substance as God, or only of similar substance. There were some heretical movements which attempted to mitigate the doctrine. Many of the bishops who participated at that council were old men, lame and disfigured from the persecutions of the Roman Emperor Diocletian. The issue was a vital one for them, because they had all testified to its truth at great personal cost to themselves. They had seen parents, relatives, friends and brother-priests persecuted and killed for their faith in the divinity of Christ. This was the faith they had inherited from their forefathers. They knew what had been believed from the beginning by thousands upon thousands of Christians. When Diocletian demanded a renunciation of Christ's divinity, hundreds of thousands went to their death in a most cruel fashion, rather than deny this belief.

The formulation of this dogma was more than an exercise in theology; it was a living act of faithfulness to the word made flesh. The faith of the Church was then sealed in words in the formula of the Nicean Creed. Its doctrinal formulation declaring Christ's true divinity was the product of more than 300 years of costly faith.

This very Creed is recited as a profession of faith after the gospel at mass in Catholic worship every Sunday, and in many Protestant churches, too. Christ is acclaimed:

God from God, light from light, true God from true God: begotten not made, one in substance with the father.

The Greeks and Roman pagans of the early era of Christian history were not so much perturbed by the idea that God could take a human form; after all, this is how they depicted their own gods, but they were absolutely startled by the idea that Christians actually believed in a supreme being who was willing to surrender his power and suffer an ignominious death for mankind. That was absurd. But Christians did not believe it was absurd. Too many of them died for it. They believed that God laid down his life for them. Their whole faith, life and dedication became a response to this extraordinary truth. God became a man like us in all things but sin. All of human nature, with its weaknesses and proclivity to evil, was ennobled and dignified by the intimate touch of the divine presence.

The Faith Experience of Christians

The Christian is one who affirms the reality and dignity of his own human nature, precisely because of the reality and dignity of Jesus Christ, the second person of the Trinity, who assumed a human nature and loved it. He loved all those who possess such a nature even to the point of giving himself in the only way men can measure total love, by giving himself unto death.

The New Testament has much to offer on the meaning of the incarnation.

> He is the image of the invisible God,
> the first-born of all creation;
> for in him all things were created.
> (Col. 1: 15-16)

> Though he was in the form of God,
> he did not count equality with God
> a thing to be grasped,
> but emptied himself,
> taking the form of a servant
> being born in the likeness of men.
> (Phil. 2: 6,7)

In the beginning was the Word
and the Word was with God,
and the Word was God.
He was in the beginning with God.
(Jn. 1: 1-2)

All things were made through him,
and without him was not made
anything that was made.
(Jn. 1:3)

All things were created through him
and for him.
(Col. 1:16)

Once the realization of who he was is grasped, his message becomes all the more important. Christ spoke frequently about his mission among men to announce the coming of the kingdom.

Then turning to the disciples he said privately, "Blessed are the eyes which see what you see! For I tell you that many prophets and kings desired to see what you see, and did not see it, and to hear what you hear, and did not hear it." (Lk. 10: 23-24)

And again:

"Blessed is he who takes no offence at me." (Mt. 11:6)

"The kingdom of heaven is like treasure hidden in a field, which a man found and covered up; then in his joy he goes and sells all that he has and buys that field." (Mt. 13:44)

"The kingdom of heaven is like leaven which a woman took and hid in three measures of meal, till it all was leavened." (Mt. 13:33)

"The kingdom of heaven is like a grain of mustard seed which a man took and sowed in his field; it is the smallest of all seeds, but when it has grown it is the greatest of shrubs and becomes a tree, so that the birds of the air come and make nests in its branches." (Mt. 13: 31-32)

"The kingdom of God is as if a man should scatter seed

upon the ground, and should sleep and rise night and day, and the seed should sprout and grow, he knows not how. The earth produces of itself, first the blade, then the ear, then the full grain in the ear. But when the grain is ripe, at once he puts in the sickle, because the harvest has come." (Mk. 4: 26-29)

The New Testament tells how Jesus, the son of God, went on to face hostility, persecution and ultimately death on the cross. Added to the claim of his divinity the gospels tell of the ignominious reality of his death, an apparent contradiction to many. To understand it one must understand more about Christ.

To speak of Jesus, his life and preaching, we must also speak about the Father whom Jesus loved and worshiped. The Father was the very center of his life; he had come precisely to do the Father's will. Indeed it was the Father's will that Jesus should undergo the agony and death of a common criminal.

Jesus' prayer was always directed to the Father, his energy always spent in the mission given to him by the Father. He prepared for the public ministry by going into the desert to pray. He took moments and hours of refuge in isolation from other men to commune with the Father. He prayed the night before choosing his apostles. His miracles were accomplished after praying to the Father. Perhaps the most moving of his prayers came the night before he died when Jesus prayed for his Church. This beautiful plea to the Father, the quintessence of Jesus' prayer is presented in the gospel according to John.

"Now, Father, it is time for you to glorify me with that glory I had with you before the world was. I have made your name known to men you took from the world to give to me. They were yours and you gave them to me, and they have kept your word.

Now at last they know that all you have given me comes indeed from you, for I have given them the teaching you gave to me.

I pray for them. I am not praying for the world but for those you have given me, because they belong to you: All I have is yours and all you have is mine, and in them I am glorified. I am not in the world any longer but they are in the world and I am coming to you . . . Holy Father . . ." (Jn. 17, 5-11)

Christ calls Almighty God "Father." Literally, "Abba," a word which conveys a far more intimate relationship than our translation. "Abba" in Aramaic is a diminutive form of a familiar address and might be rendered in colloquial English as "Poppa" or "Daddy," the first utterance of a child to his father. It is the same father whom Jesus taught his followers to address in the Lord's Prayer. Christians are invited by Christ to address the Father with the same childlike abandonment, the same simple dependency. Christ delivered up his life to the Father: "Abba, Abba, into your hands I commend my Spirit."

In the final scene of the Gospel story Jesus is raised by the Father from the dead. From the very beginning of Christianity there was this overwhelming certainty in the community of the faithful that Jesus was resurrected. This belief and conviction was the foundation and power thrust of the Church's early preaching, "If Christ has not been raised, then our preaching is empty and your faith without foundation . . . your faith is futile and you are still in your sins." (1 Cor. 15: 14,17)

There is no scientific evidence of his resurrection, no first-hand witness of the event itself, but the Gospels contain accounts of Christ's appearances to Mary, to Peter and the Apostles, and then to the large community of disciples. The themes presented are the same in all the accounts, an empty tomb, the appearance of angels, the presence of a living Christ. But another miracle more possible to grasp is that Christians have died by the hundreds of thousands for this faith, not in a spirit of dejection and resignation, but in a joyful triumphalism which has echoed through the centuries in every Easter celebration, in the celebration of every Sunday Mass and every other worship service in Christendom. This joy is an inexpressible expanse of vision and heart which comes from a knowledge that sins are forgiven; sorrow and pain are wiped away; good triumphs over evil; and that God, the giver of all good gifts, is reckless in his love for man. The crucifix paradoxically is a demonstration of the passion and totality of this love.

Three Persons, One God

The doctrine of the Trinity is the chief obstacle for most non-Christians in the acceptance of Christianity. Christians believe in one God, but he is described as three distinct persons in one being. The mathematical formula—three equals one—is difficult for any mind to grasp, so it is no wonder that many find it unacceptable. However, Christians have experienced God in their own unique way, and that experience is extremely important in their understanding of God.

A brief review of the Jewish Bible is needed to understand revelation as it is developed in the New Testament. The ancient Jews spoke poetically of God in many ways, but two dominant themes manifest themselves continually. They knew God could never be understood or visualized, but they made repeated references to his presence as the mysterious "breath of life" and as the spoken "word" at the beginning of creation.

> In the beginning God created the earth and sky. Now the world was empty and formless with darkness hanging over deep waters. But the breath of God stirred the waters. God gave the word, "Let there be light." And there was light. (Gen. 1:1-3)

The word was spoken and there was light. The same theme is repeated in the familiar account of the creation of man.

> Yahweh shaped man from the clay of the earth and breathed into his nostrils the breath of life, and man became a living being. (Gen. 2:7)

The breath of God was understood as that life-giving power which came from God's very being. His word was understood as power itself, commanding, creating and recreating the universe. God spoke the word through the prophets. Ezechiel's preaching is an example of divine intercession in establishing a new Israel.

> He said to me, "Son of man, all these bones represent the people of Israel. They have been saying, 'Our bones are dried up, our hope is lost, we have been cut off from our destiny!'" So he told me, "Preach to those bones: You dry bones, hear the word of the Lord! This is what the Lord God says to you bones: I am going to breathe into you and you will live!" (Ez. 11)

If it was understood that God acted in history through his breath and through his word, it is not difficult to see how the early Christian community began to see a deeper meaning in the words of Christ.

> The things I do in my Father's name are my witnesses . . . The Father and I are one. (Jn. 10:25)

But when He, the Spirit of Truth has come, He will teach you all the truth. For he will not speak on his own authority but whatever He will hear He will speak, and the things that are to come He will declare to you. (Jn. 16:13)

Jesus taught by his presence that there was a unity between the word God spoke and the breath he breathed, and a distinction as well. The early Christian community began to examine their own experience of God's revelation to them, and they understood Jesus as the word of God:

And the Word became man and made His home among us. (Jn. 4:14)

The breath of Yahweh was now not merely a divine attribute, an extension of God's power, but the advocate, a distinct and separate person within the Godhead, descending upon the apostles at Pentecost, filling the Church with new life, renewing the face of the earth. God's word was experienced personally through, with, and in Jesus. God's breath was experienced in the coming of the Spirit at Pentecost and throughout the history of the Church. The intimate union, while maintaining the distinction between the three, is described by Christians as a mystery. One either accepts it, or one rejects it.

It may be interesting to note here that for the Hindu, God is described in a variety of ways. He is referred to as "Brahman," and the many faces of Brahman include a trinitarian formula: Brahman the creator, Vishnu the preserver and Shiva the destroyer. This is a thoroughly different notion of God than perceived in Christian revelation, but it is nevertheless interesting to see that a religion, more ancient than

Christianity and Judaism, contains an expression of God formulated in terms of a trinity.

Christian Asceticism

All Christians are called by Christ to be perfect. "Be you therefore perfect as also your heavenly Father is perfect" (Matt. 5:48). In considering what he meant by these words we find an extraordinary level of expectation. "Turn the other cheek to one who slaps your face; he who would take away your coat, let him have your cloak also. Love your enemies, do good to them that hate you, and pray for them that persecute and calumniate you" (Matt. 5:44). Christ asked for a degree of perfection seldom found in daily life.

Even in his last prayer at the first eucharistic banquet: "Not for them only do I pray, but for them also who through their word shall believe in me. That they all may be one, as Thou Father in me, and I in Thee . . . that they may be made perfectly one" (Jn. 17: 20, 21, 23). Christ is calling for a perfection in which the soul is assimilated into the life of the Trinity. This was not intended merely for popes, bishops and priests, but for all men, women and children, who through the teachings of the apostles would believe in Christ throughout the ages. The love of God is the essence of Christian perfection.

St. Thomas Aquinas put it simply: "The perfection of Christian life consists fundamentally and essentially in charity manifesting itself mainly in the love of God, and, secondarily, in the love of our neighbor."

The summit of Christian perfection to which Christians themselves are called can be reached only in heaven. Only here will the Christian comprehend how small and insignificant his human efforts have been in attaining this sublime goal; only in heaven will he properly understand how much he needed in the way of divine assistance. Nevertheless, there are definite means for attaining holiness, and these are the same ones which are available to every member of the Church, priest, religious or layman.

The ordinary means of attaining sanctity are prayer, charitable actions, the practice of self-denial, and the sacraments, particularly the eucharist which for Christians is Christ's gift of himself under the appearance of bread and wine. These serve to help Christians in the loving fulfillment of the duties of their individual state in life. All Christians are thus called to the summit of perfection and share the same means to sanctity. There is no difference in the tools used, but certain differences do arise among priests and the laity, monks and nuns, and other religious, in the way they make use of the ordinary means of spiritual discipline.

Monasticism tends to stress group living and group participation in the practices of the spiritual life within the framework of obedience to the rules of the community. Those not bound in the religious vows of poverty, chastity and obedience, including priests and the laity, strive for holiness without group identification.

All of the founders of religious orders, the monks and hermits of Christian antiquity have pursued the goal of perfect charity through various forms of self-discipline. Celibacy was praised and practiced from the beginning because Christ both praised and practiced it. It is an extraordinary means of attaining holiness.

Throughout the two thousand years of Christianity, Catholics have depended for their strength and

sustenance on Christ in the eucharist. The Mass is the
highest form of Catholic worship. Saints, scholars and
sinners and all combinations thereof, have been
nourished spiritually by this mystery of faith. The Mass
with its four elements: communion, sacrifice, eucharist
and memorial, has within it five purposes, or effects:
namely, adoration (*latreia*), thanksgiving (*eucharistia*),
prayer (*impetratio*), forgiveness (*propitiatio*) and satis-
faction for sins (*satisfactio*).

All of this theological categorization should at
least suggest the complexity of the subject. Nevertheless, the most simple peasant has attended Mass with
devotion and has understood the miracle of Christ's
coming in the eucharist as a genuine feeding of his
lambs and his sheep. The Lamb of God, Jesus, the victim for man's sins, is offered to the Father at each
Mass. In his self-giving he takes away the sins of the
world. Popes and farmers, monks and housewives, have
all based their spirituality on the eucharist.

The following poetic tribute to the Mass by Catherine de Vinck captures beautifully its sweeping drama.

We come to you Father
With praise and thanksgiving;
Through Jesus Christ Your Son we ask you
To accept and bless these gifts.

We come to you
Through a wilderness of silence
Our thoughts moving wordlessly
Tracing a new of random trails.
It is cold in the land:

>   the key of winter
>   turns in the lock
>   of earth, of water.

The garden which was rich with apple
>   with calling bird and growing plant
>   sours and freezes.

—All the chains of emotions and feelings
All efforts to meet, touch, talk,
            perish
Trapped in the ice of our wintering—
We walk till we come
            to the end of the world
               end of time
               end of thought,
Exhausted, dumb creatures
Lost in the confusion of tongues.
What language shall we speak?
What word shall be the diamond
       to cut the glass, break the ice
       release the flow of life?

GOD
      You are everywhere
                        anywhere
                                  nowhere

        to be seen.
Out of the chambers and streets
          of many lives, of many years
We come
          preciously holding what we saved:
A little wheel of bread
Image of the endless circling of our hungers,
A splash of wine
In a cup where the sun of all our thirsts
trembles and shines. . . .

TAKE AND EAT: THIS IS MY BODY.

He makes the time
                improvises the place:
He speaks himself
              into earth
                  water
                  air
                  fire.
Under nail and thorn
Under rod and spear
They scream
            the four elements of His mastering.

In its cave the heart weeps
Not tears but healing fluids
Bright semen, seeds of worlds to be.
Do we know the tidings? See
the final shape of all that fluctuates
between birth and death?
Forms in fusion, chanced words
become safe and solid vehicles
Carriers of love.

Look
     at the rose—real,
     real rose blooming marvelously,
     taking space
     in the narrow realness of our gazing.

Enclosed
     We are enclosed
     Having no more than the eye
     to see, missing
     what most really appears
     beyond our sight.

He marks the time
     improvises the place
     speaks himself alive
     in a flake of bread.

TAKE AND DRINK: THIS IS MY BLOOD.

We die of thirst by the sea-mouth
      —O bitter water—
We die of thirst by the streams and waterfalls
      —O beautiful water-lights
        silver and amber rings
        locked circles in which we drown—
Our private human paths twist
Like ropes through stubble fields
and the dust rises, the tree sleeps
without greening.
Our human words turn
      always at the same angle
        —not knowing how
         not knowing why—
      return to the same stillness.

But He breaks the silence
His voice cutting clear through

the countries of the past;
A stream flowing through the rock
in time
out of time
Flooding the depth of our need
—O sweet and saving rain
that soaks the roots of our desire
Wakes the dormant seeds
of the Holy of Eden—

Let us proclaim the mystery of faith:
CHRIST HAS DIED
CHRIST IS RISEN
CHRIST WILL COME AGAIN.

QUESTIONS TO THINK ABOUT

1. Do you think belief in the incarnation affects the way a Christian regards other humans and himself? Explain your answer.

2. Christianity has been described as a religion of paradoxes: discovering life in death, wealth in poverty, strength through weakness, etc. Do you think this way of looking at things is useful for modern people, or useless?

3. Christian spirituality has been described as the striving for personal perfection. One gospel story relates Jesus' advice to a young man: "If you would be perfect, go, sell what you possess and give to the poor, and you will have treasure in heaven; and come, follow me" (Matt. 19:21). For you is this advice realistic or unrealistic, appealing or unappealing?

6
ISLAM

A Muslim is a follower of Mohammed. The religion of Mohammed is more properly called Islam, rather than Mohammedanism.

At the turn of the sixth century after Christ, this young man named Mohammed was seen daily ascending Mount Hera, a barren mountain on the outskirts of Mecca. In a small cave he would pray and meditate alone for hours. A momentous struggle was taking place within his soul, a struggle born of spiritual hunger. The world he grew up in was a chaotic one, filled with superstitious fears. Desert spirits and minor deities, called Jinn, abounded. The people formed a multitude of contentious tribes, each with its own gods, its own language and dress.

For years Mohammed would go to his mountain to pray, returning home each day to his wife Khadija who is remembered for the encouragement she gave him during this long period of soul-searching. It was to Khadija that he first confided his belief that God was speaking to him through the Angel Gabriel. He was to proclaim Allah to the world as the one true God.

The Message of Allah

In the polytheistic city of Mecca, proclamation of Allah as the only God was a declaration of war on the ancient loyalties of a passionate people. Mohammed was born about 570 A.D. in Mecca, a city in western Saudi Arabia. His father died before his birth and his mother died before he was seven. He was raised by an uncle, Abu-Talib, who prepared him for a career in business. Traveling in camel caravans loaded with handmade objects from Mecca, Mohammed learned to trade in the foreign markets of Egypt and Palestine. His early travels brought him in contact with Christians and Jews. He became fascinated with their religious heritage. As a young man he was well experienced in the business world and obtained employment as a chief steward for a very rich widow. Though she was much older than he, they eventually married. It was her wealth and her love which later enabled him to pursue a life of solitude.

As his mission became increasingly clear, he began to venture into public places and preach the revelations from Allah. Fierce opposition met him at every turn, not only from the leaders of established religious sects, but also from local business men in Mecca who lived off the shrines and pilgrims. To complicate the matter, each shrine proclaimed a local deity. Allah had been known merely as one of the local gods who lived at Mount Hera. For Mohammed to announce the god of Mount Hera as the only God, was to cancel in one stroke the validity of all other shrines. This alone was enough to put his life in danger, but he outfoxed his enemies through an unbelievable series of events which began with his flight from Mecca. He escaped to Yathrib, later called Medina, a city about 270 miles north of Mecca, and there preached the same message. For the first three years he was able to attract only 40 or so followers, but by the time of his death in 632 A.D., he had amassed an army of followers.

Mohammed was honest about his mission. Even when his disciples wanted to make an idol of him, he would resist them: "God has not sent me to work wonders; he has sent me to preach . . . I never said that Allah's treasures are in my hand, that I knew the hidden things or that I was an angel . . . I am only a preacher of God's words." But he remembered bitterly those who rejected and spurned him, those who drove him at swordpoint from Mecca, the home of his birth.

The actual flight from Mecca, which is called the Hegira, took place in 622 A.D., and is now celebrated annually as a sacred day for Muslims throughout the world. The Hegira is the point in time which Muslims use to reckon their calendar. Christians might better appreciate the meaning of the phenomenal rise of Islam if they understood the struggle of Mohammed against his adversaries.

He was a revolutionary, not merely on the theological level, but on the economic and racial level as well. His theory of monotheism called into question all the established religious theories of his day. For generations families made their living from the shrines attached to the various gods. One temple in Mecca alone had a shrine for every day of the year. He preached loud and clear: "There is only one God, his name is Allah, and I, Mohammed, am his greatest prophet." All the shrines were disfigured by his frightful words.

In the beginning he was hesitant and unsure of himself about the idea that God had actually chosen him to preach this message, but his faith grew and his devoted wife reassured him that his private visions were from God.

There is no denying that he eventually brought his people from a primitive form of religion to a highly refined sense of God, but in the beginning his preaching caused havoc in the marketplace. It repudiated the devotional practices of thousands upon thousands of local Arabs. He further infuriated the already hostile crowds by preaching the equality of all men. In fact, the women's liberation movement received one of its first major boosts from this man. He resisted the social pattern of the day which supported the subjugation of women and enabled the upper classes to exploit and manipulate the poor. Daughters were usually unwanted and always omitted from the inheritance which their brothers divided. Mohammed fought for their rights, outraging the stubborn, selfish male population. He preached this rigid moral code and he raised the hatred of an entire city. But he preached his message; and even in flight persisted to win followers. In a few short years he managed to take over political leadership of Medina and he prepared an army to return and capture Mecca. His series of military victories made a colossal impact on the Arabs of his day and they saw him as God's chosen warrior. He won adherents to the faith of Islam all over the Arab world. His movement spread rapidly for a hundred years after his death. Had not the Muslim armies been defeated by Emperor Charles Martel centuries later in the classic battle of Tours, Islam might have become the faith of Europe.

What Muslims Believe

The extent of Abraham's influence in the world of religion is not fully realized by most people. He is not only the father of the Jewish faith and therefore by virtue of Christ's messianic fulfillment of the Old Testament, the father of the Christian faith, but according to Mohammed himself, Abraham is also the father of the Muslim faith.

Mecca is the holy city of Islam. After Mecca and Medina, Jerusalem is Islam's third most important city, but it has the second most important Muslim temple, the Dome of the Rock. This beautiful golden dome is directly above a huge rock which enshrines the spot where Abraham is said to have brought his son Isaac to be sacrificed. This is also the site where Solomon's temple once stood, the same temple to which Christ was dragged the night before he died. The Abraham-Isaac story enshrined in a Muslim temple might surprise a few Jews and Christians, but it is a well-known fact to the followers of Islam.

Abraham came from a land where men were mere playthings of the gods; natural calamities were interpreted as the anger of the gods. To this day we call them acts of God; then they were understood as the revenge of the deities. Abraham was not conditioned to think of God as kind and loving.

The real significance of God's intervention to spare Isaac was that Abraham learned dramatically for the first time in his life that his God was a God of kindness. Isaac was saved from being sacrificed and God revealed himself as a God of love. This was the most powerful insight into God's personal nature given to man since the beginning of time.

Muslim allegiance to Abraham is based on the same Old Testament scripture. Mohammed, who began his public ministry nearly 620 years after Christ, was influenced by both the New and the Old Testament in writing the *Koran*, which is the Bible of Islam.

In the Jewish Bible Mohammed read the story of

Abraham, his wife Sara and his slave girl Agar. In that
story, Agar became pregnant by Abraham, and feeling
her womanly pride at bearing the offspring of her master, she began to humiliate his wife Sara who was barren. Sara complained to Abraham about it, and he gave
Sara permission to deal with Agar as she saw fit. Sara
mistreated the slave girl who eventually ran away. In
the wilderness, an angel of the Lord came to Agar and
told her to return to Abraham, promising, "I will mul-
tiply thy seed exceedingly . . . thou art with child and
thou shalt bring forth a son, and thou shalt call his
name Ismael, because the Lord has heard thy affliction" (Gen. 16: 10,11).

She did return and gave birth to Ismael who grew
up in the presence of Abraham. Eventually Ismael went
down to the land of Egypt to settle there and it is from
his offspring that Mohammed and his followers claim
direct lineage with Abraham. The Muslims have much
in common with the Judaic-Christian traditions. However, Mohammed claimed that Christ was merely
God's servant, a prophet, but not equal to Allah. Mary,
who is mentioned respectfully thirty-four times in the
Koran, is referred to as the mother of Christ, never the
mother of God. The Trinity is rejected:

> They surely disbelieve who say: "Behold, Allah is the
> Messiah, son of Mary . . . Allah is the third of three,"
> when there is no god save the One God. (*Koran*)

Mohammed made it very clear that certain things
were expected of his followers. There are Five Pillars of
the Islam faith, which are five principles given to Mohammed to regulate a Muslim's religious life. The first
pillar has to do with his creed; it is a very simple creed
that is phrased in the following words: "There is no

God but Allah, and Mohammed is his prophet." Every Muslim must make this act of faith at least once in a lifetime, but as a practical matter a good Muslim will repeat it many times a day.

The second pillar is prayer. In order to keep his life in close contact with God and be faithful to the Koran which urges him to "be constant" in prayer, he bows low before his maker, expresses his creaturehood and submits himself to the will of God. He does this five times a day, at rising, at noon, in mid-afternoon, after sunset and before retiring. The routine is flexible and subject to adjustment, if circumstances demand it. If a traveler is by the roadside at sunset, it is taught in the Koran that Allah's universe is entirely pure and the faithful are to spread their prayer rug anywhere they find themselves at the appointed hour.

In Arab countries it is a common thing to see Muslims wash their feet before prayer to purify themselves, expressing their desire to be worthy and clean in God's sight. Muslims face Mecca when they pray, not only to express their solidarity with their brothers all over the world who are doing the same thing at the same time, but also to revere the Holy City where Mohammed received his revelation and preached the messages of the glories of Allah.

The prayers contain praise, gratitude and petition. There are a variety of prayers which might be said. The following set is an example:

Thanks be to my Lord: He the Adorable, and only to be adored. My Lord, the Eternal, the Ever-existing, the Cherisher, the True Sovereign whose mercy and might overshadow the universe: the Regulator of the world, and Light of the creation. His is our worship: to Him belongs all worship: He existed before all things, and will exist after all that is living has ceased. Thou art the adored,

my Lord: Thou art the Master, the Loving and Forgiving
. . . Thou art the Helper of the Afflicted, the Reliever of
all distress, the Consoler of the brokenhearted: Thou art
present everywhere to help Thy servants . . . O my
Lord, Thou art the Creator. I am only created: Thou art
my Sovereign, I am only Thy servant: Thou art the
Helper, I am the beseecher: Thou are the Forgiver, I am
the sinner: Thou, my Lord, art the Merciful, All-Know-
ing, All-Loving . . . O Lord, grant to me the love of
Thee. Grant that I may love those that love Thee. Grant
that I may do the deeds that win Thy love. Make Thy
love to be dearer to me than self, family or than wealth.
O Lord: Grant me firmness in faith and direction. Assist
me in being grateful to Thee and in adoring Thee in
every good way. I ask Thee for an innocent heart, which
shall not incline to wickedness. I ask Thee for a true
tongue, I pray Thee to defend me from that vice which
Thou knowest, and for forgiveness of those faults which
Thou knowest. O my Defender: Assist me in remembering Thee and being grateful to Thee, and in worshiping
Thee with the excess of my strength. Forgive me out of
Thy loving kindness, and have mercy on me: for verily
Thou art the forgiver of offences and the bestower of
blessings on Thy servants.

The third pillar of Islam is the month-long fast.
Once a year during the ninth month of the Islamic calendar which is called Ramadan, a strict fast is enjoined.
No food or drink, tobacco or sexual intercourse is allowed from sun-up to sunset. For the Arab people,
rooted in arid land as they are, this month of fasting is
an extraordinary sacrifice. The two principal feast days
of the year are the Lesser Festival, the feast of Break-
ing of the Fast of Ramadan, and the Greater Festival,
the Feast of Sacrifice.

At the end of Ramadan a three-day celebration
begins with morning prayers, usually out in the open.
They pray for good health, good crops, forgiveness of
sins and safety from bad luck, as the festival begins.
Grudges are forgotten, enemies are reconciled, alms are

given to the poor, and the hunger of the long fast is satisfied by three days of eating and rejoicing.

The fourth pillar of Islam is almsgiving. Mohammed required his followers to distribute to the poor each year, two-and-a-half percent of their entire holdings. That means that a Muslim is expected to give away one-fortieth of everything he owns once every twelve months. While it is obvious that all Muslims do not fulfill this prescript to the letter of the law, most of them do. In fact, they usually do it in bits and pieces all year around. The poor share their meager food supply with their neighbors, or give freely of their own labor to help their neighbor in distress.

The fifth pillar of Islam is the pilgrimage to Mecca. If possible this should be made at least once in a lifetime. Elaborate ritual purifications are required before the pilgrim enters Mecca. The men shave their heads and the women cover their heads. No fasting is necessary in Mecca for the pilgrimage, but sexual intercourse and the use of perfume are forbidden. Making the pilgrimage is not an absolute requirement for salvation, but it is a sure sign of fidelity to the will of Allah. Very often the pilgrims are tattooed on their faces and hands to show that they have made the sacred journey.

The biggest celebration of the Muslim year, the Great Festival, is held on the Day of Sacrifice, which is the last day of the pilgrimage to Mecca. Every Muslim all over the world shares in the celebration. It begins with common prayers in the open. The father of the family takes the animal dedicated for sacrifice, a sheep, goat, cow or camel. The head of the animal is turned toward Mecca and it is killed while ritual prayers are recited. One-third of the flesh is given to the poor, one-third to the relatives, and one-third is used for the family feast. The festival lasts for three days. This sacrifice commemorates Abraham's willingness to offer his beloved son. This offering of a slain victim to the Father is similar in essence to the Catholic Mass which is an offering of the crucified victim, Jesus Christ, to the Father under the appearance of bread and wine. The Muslims, however, do not advert to Christ in their Great Festival on the Day of Sacrifice.

The Piety of Islam

The *Koran* is the Bible of Islam. It has 114 chapters arranged according to their length, the shortest being first. The whole text is prefaced by the opening Surah which became the model of Islamic prayer:

> Praise be to God, Lord of
> the world;
> The Compassionate, the merciful
> King on the day of reckoning:
> Thee only do we worship, and
> to Thee do we cry for help.
> Guide Thou us on the straight
> path, the path of those to whom
> Thou has been gracious:
> With whom Thou are not angry,
> and who do not stray.

Mohammed claimed that the Angel Gabriel actually wrote the *Koran* and dictated it to him word for word. His communications with the Archangel are supposed to have lasted for a period of about 22 years.

There are four fundamental beliefs in the *Koran:* (a) the world was created by Allah; (b) man is absolutely subject to the will of Allah in all things; (c) man must perform the tasks which Allah assigns to him; (d) Allah will reward good and punish evil after this life, according to the way man performs his tasks. These tasks are called the Five Pillars of Islam, which we have just reviewed. A Muslim must perform these five basic duties in life, and, if he does, he will have pleased Allah and gained a life of eternal happiness which is depicted in the *Koran* in human sensual terms.

The Orthodox Muslim takes a fundamentalistic view of the *Koran*. Every word is considered to be of divine origin. Islam also looks upon the Old and New Testaments of the Judaic-Christian heritage as authentic but incomplete revelations from God. The fullness of revelation is found in the *Koran* alone.

The only miracle attributed to Mohammed is the actual writing of the *Koran*. He was an uneducated peasant who could hardly sign his own name, yet he produced a book of wisdom that has moved the hearts and minds of millions upon millions of his followers for generations. The literal interpretation of the *Koran* often engenders in the Muslim a fierce legalistic spirit. The *Koran* not only approves divorce and polygamy, but it seems to encourage military power as a weapon to achieve its goals. The combination of legalism and militarism has often led to violence and bloodshed in the name of Allah.

This doesn't sound very other-worldly, does it? And yet, it's not so simple to categorize any religion, for each faith has within it currents and counter-currents. Within the first century after Mohammed there were preachers and ascetics who reacted against the materialism and political power associated with the religion. The influence of Christian asceticism, the hermits, the contemplatives, the celibates, all had an impact on Muslim teachers.

Though Mohammed denounced celibacy as an abuse of Christ's teachings, by the third century of the Muslim era a group who were identified by their garments of undyed wool (*suf*) began to challenge orthodoxy's hold over the common people. The Sufis, as they were called, eventually introduced liturgical ceremonies and a whole new attitude toward the *Koran*. Instead of fidelity to the word alone, they taught that direct, personal experience of Allah was possible, so that wisdom comes not only from the *Koran*, but from Allah's inspiration. By the fifth century the Sufis, whose most praiseworthy leaders were unmarried, were extolling celibacy.

By the eleventh century, the great Al-Ghazali (1058-1111), the Muslim equivalent of St. Augustine, synthesized the whole Sufi movement, paving the way for its acceptance by orthodoxy. To believe that God supplied religious knowledge apart from the Word of God in the *Koran* gave authority to countless religious practices not enumerated in the Holy Book. Eventually conservative forces regained control of Islam. Among the upper classes a fundamentalist approach to the *Koran* has been maintained, but to this day Sufism continues to be responsible for a wide diversity of devotions and practices which are truly Islamic but not prescribed by Mohammed.

The *Koran* offers almost nothing regarding the techniques of prayer, the way one should go about praying. Mohammed did direct his followers to face Mecca during the time of prayer but the positions of the body have developed through tradition. "Perform the prayer at the sinking of the sun to the darkening of the night and the recital of dawn."

Christian baptism has had an influence on the

Muslim custom of washing before prayer. Muslims usually begin prayer by washing their feet and spreading a prayer-rug. Many of them stand erect with their hands on each side of their face, palms open with thumbs touching their earlobes.

They then pray, "Allahu Akbar" (which means "God is most great"). The *Koran* is opened to recite the beginning *Surah* which we have seen above. Then, bowing from their waist and with hands on knees, they say: "I extol the perfection of my Lord the Great." Standing up again, "Allahu Akbar" is repeated as they slip slowly to a kneeling position from which they bow, touching the ground with the palms and forehead. Rising again to a kneeling position, they sit back on their heels and repeat the profound bow once again, touching the ground with forehead and hands. This is done five or six times while optional prayers are recited. The creed is often repeated during these exercises.

The prayerfulness of the Muslim does not remove him from the harsh realities of human conflict. The following words of Mohammed explain this ambivalence quite clearly:

> Warfare is ordained for you, though it is hateful unto you, but it may happen that you hate a thing which is good for you, and it may happen that you love a thing which is bad for you. Allah knoweth, ye know not . . . Persecution is worse than killing. And they will not cease from fighting against you till they have made you renegades from your religion, if they can. And whoso becometh a renegade and dieth in his disbelief, such are they whose works have fallen both in the world and the Hereafter. Such are rightful owners of the Fire; they will abide therein. . . .
> Fight in the way of Allah, against those who fight against you, but do not begin hostilities. Allah loveth no aggressors. And slay them wherever ye find them, and drive them out of the places whence they drove you

out. . . . If they attack you, then slay them. Such is the
reward of disbelievers.

The Muslim sense of justice is vivid not only with
respect to enemies but also in matters of social thought.
Without a doubt his social theory hit the tribal civilization of his day with the force of a sonic boom. His
social doctrine broke new ground in three areas: economics, women, and race relations.

Economics: Mohammed tried to instill a social
consciousness among the faithful. In his day, men and
women were victimized by severe poverty and injustice,
living under rigid caste systems. Mohammed taught
that wealth should be widely distributed and shared
with the less fortunate. His device for accomplishing
this was basically the fourth pillar of Islam, where one-
fortieth of one's income is pledged for redistribution
among the poorer elements of society.

Women: There are different opinions about Mohammed's attitude toward women. He is criticized for
promoting a man's world by allowing a plurality of
wives. This practice, though degrading to women in our
culture, was the common practice for wealthy Arabs.
Mohammed did stress the dignity and equality of
women in this set of traditions. He rejected the prevalent idea that women were property, that baby daughters were valueless. He forbade infanticide and demanded an equal inheritance for all children. The Koran
opens the way for a fuller equality of women and men
in education, voting and professional life, though many
centuries of the patriarchical domination have dimmed
the actual progress of women in most areas of the Arab
world.

Mohammed forbade sexual promiscuity outside of

marriage and in this teaching alone protected women from the extreme abuses of a primitive society. He sanctified marriage and raised women to a level of dignity that was unknown in the ancient Arabic-speaking world. Remember, this was a world where a father might sell his daughter to the highest bidder to be used as the buyer chose to use her.

Race Relations: Not only did Mohammed insist on complete equality among the races, but he even encouraged and praised intermarriage as the greatest sign of interracial love and harmony. One of his wives was a Negro, and his own daughter married a Negro. The Black Muslim movement in the United States is considered heretical by orthodox Islamic teachers precisely because it is racially selective and discriminatory, a stance which Mohammed would condemn as evil.

QUESTIONS TO THINK ABOUT

1. On the basis of what you know, what do you find attractive in the faith of Islam? What attitudes do you have in common with Muslims?

2. In what way does religion bring order into a world of chaos? Give examples.

3. How successful would you be in keeping the Five Pillars of the Islamic faith? Would you like to try? (Of course you would have to choose another city of pilgrimage instead of Mecca, where only Muslims may dwell.) What affect do you think the observance of these tasks would have on you?

7
HINDUISM

Hinduism, the world's most ancient religion, and the third largest of all religions, is really not a religion at all. In fact it is more like an amalgamation of three different historical traditions, united by a geographical location and a common sacred culture. Hinduism is so named because it is the religion of India, the land around the Indus river, but there are many Hindus also in Burma and Ceylon. Hinduism remained localized in Southern Asia until modern times when the influence of the guru touched the Western world. Through mass media we learned that even the Beatles went to India to learn the secrets of contemplation.

The Emergence of Hinduism

Hinduism has no historical founder. Its origins reach back to primitive antiquity. Part of the secret of Hinduism's syncretist character stems from its evolution since 1500 B.C. Around that time Aryan tribesmen invaded the Punjab from the north. They brought with them their own faith. This was the first of the three traditions which fused with primitive animism. The spirit of the period is expressed in a collection of hymns called the *Rig Veda*. It is made up of animistic songs and prayers personifying nature, attributing divine personalities to the forces of fire, thunder, sunshine, rain, etc. The *Rig Veda* is also a ritual of primitive spells and charms. During this period the religion of India was called Vedaism. Hinduism had not yet evolved.

The *Rig Veda* shows no signs of a belief in reincarnation or caste systems. It is basically the song book of the Ancient Aryans—barbaric, crude and lusty. Gradually, after a period of about 500 years, the Aryans moved from the desert-like Punjab to the valley of the Ganges, where the land was green with lush vegetation. In five centuries, people change; the sacred writings of the *Rig Veda* became obsolete and had to be reinterpreted. The archaic language needed updating. The second stage of India's religious development began during this transition period. A class of learned commentators arose, the forerunners of the priestly caste, and they began to write their thoughts and comments on the sacred book.

Two kinds of literature developed: the ritual books called *Brahmanas* and the commentaries called *Upanishad*. The *Brahmanas* made the priestly caste indispensable for salvation, insisting on exact fidelity to the written law. The *Upanishads* stressed the importance of each individual's personal effort in attaining salvation, stressing the need for contemplation and ascetical practices more than dependence on the priests. These works date back to the golden age of India between 1000 B.C. and 500 B.C., and they reveal a movement away from the polytheistic worship of individual deities to the monotheistic worship of the one who is all, the Brahman.

The Brahman is the central theological idea in both of these later writings. Brahman is the one, unifying, omnipresent God of the universe. Eventually these two literary trends overshadowed the *Rig Veda* and Vedaism gradually became Brahmanism.

Soon after a multiplicity of minor sects began to appear, variations on the theme of Brahmanism. This wide diversity of philosophical offshoots gradually became what we now know as modern Hinduism. Eliot, in his book, *Hinduism and Buddhism*, said that there was no way to describe the incredible complexity of Hinduism, "the same religion enjoins self-mortification and orgies; commands human sacrifices and yet counts it a sin to crush an insect or eat meat; has more priests, rites and images than ancient Egypt or medieval Rome, and yet outdoes Quakers in rejecting all externals."

The *Ramayans* and the *Mahabharata* which contain the well-known *Bhagavad Gita* represent the wearisome literature of this period of early Hindu development.

Hinduism differs from Brahmanism in that it is more human and down-to-earth, less esoteric and less inhibited. Brahman is still the all-pervading center, the totality of all that is, but in practice the Hindu is attracted to him under one or another of his manifestations, particularly Vishnu, the savior of man. Vishnu is believed to have walked the earth in human form many times in the history of the world. Because of this Hindus have no difficulty with the idea of an incarnation and most of them could easily accept Jesus Christ as an authentic incarnation of the Brahman.

The spirit of openness in Hinduism is the key to understanding the tolerance found in this amazing diversity of beliefs. The Hindu accepts every religious sensitivity as coming from Brahman. Since everything is viewed as a passing manifestation of the one underlying unity which is the Brahman, who is the "all," the totality of reality, nothing is really foreign or strange. This is the monist view of reality.

When Pope Paul VI made his historic visit to India, the people lined the streets by the hundreds of thousands, and they stood in silence. The pope, though deeply moved, was probably not surprised, for he knew that Hindus regard a high holy man of any religion as a visible and sacred manifestation of the great Brahman. They would not view Catholicism as a false religion, but rather as one of the many expressions of truth which flow from Brahman.

This is not to say that factionalism is absent from Hinduism—far from it. There are over 845 dialects spoken in India, creating severe communication problems, and there is an elaborate caste system rooted in racial and color differences. The caste system is closely bound up with the law of Karma. This belief in reincarnation looks at each caste as a self-contained unit, a fate determined by birth and not broken until death. Death brings either graduation to a higher state of existence in a new life, or failure and degradation to a lower state. The Untouchable is the lowest human caste, but one can descend to the animal or insect level.

Mother Teresa of India is a Catholic nun who founded a community of women dedicated to serve the poor and dying of India. There are 80 million Untouchables in India, and thousands are left to die in the streets of Calcutta. Everyone, including the Untouchables, believes they are only getting what they rightly deserve. Suffering is inevitable, and trying to relieve it is futile. This is the law of Karma. Christian charity opposes this fatalism of India rather dramatically, and the contrast is made obvious in the person of Mother Teresa as she and her followers cart the sick and dying back to their convent hospital.

The Faith of a Hindu

Brahman is the ultimate reality. The only definite thing one can say about him is that he is unknowable. For the Hindu any attempt to classify the ultimate one is foolishness. God may or may not be a person, or three persons, or a hundred persons; may or may not be a creator, father or protector. He, she or it is beyond human categorization. The great one is infinite. The unsearchable one will never be known. The ground of being "before whom all words recoil" is mystery.

A rich, almost limitless variety of conceptions have developed concerning God's nature. The Hindu truly believes that Brahman is unknowable, but there are countless sects which describe their God in a highly specific way. Some think of him as a personal God, named Saguna Brahman. This image is much like the Christian conceptualization of God: loving provident, concerned about one and all in every moment of time. Others conceive God as Nirguna Brahman, an aloof, impersonal being. For them, "God isn't dead; he just doesn't want to get involved."

Openness is the key to the diversity of Hindu belief. Every Hindu sees other sects, and other religions as expressions of truth; each one sees one of the many faces of Brahman, but no one can see the whole. Each faith is merely an attempt on the part of man to comprehend a particular aspect of God. Thus the Hindu respect for Christianity as an approach is at the same time mixed with a defiant resistance to the idea that any particular religion is the one, true religion.

The more enlightened Christian missionaries have for a long time realized that their missionary movement must accommodate itself to the Hindu spirit rather than demand a complete accommodation to one Christian church. Early missionaries from Portugal transplanted Portuguese Christianity to India. Portuguese architecture, customs and modes of piety were presented as the Christian faith. To become a Christian an Indian had to identify with a foreign culture. Obviously there was a low conversion rate in this country, and to this day the Indian government looks with suspicion on all foreign missionaries.

The limitless expressions of the great Brahman also include a Hindu trinity. God manifests himself as Brahman, the Creator; Vishnu, the Preserver, and Shiva, the Destroyer, corresponding roughly to the Christian concept of Father, Son, and Holy Spirit. Shiva, the Destroyer, controls all forces which bring living things back to the hidden center or soul of the universe. All living reality one day dies and is then absorbed back into Brahman. This idea of bringing all things back to God is also the idea or mission of the Christian Holy Spirit, although Christians conceive of the Spirit's work as creative rather than destructive.

Hinduism still contains the vestiges of polytheism, which is simply accepted as the many faces of Brahman. India is full of shrines and temples which are inhabited by one or more of the Hindu pantheon of gods. People come to the shrine not for congregational worship so much as to visit the place where their god actually dwells. This is done without denying the undivided reality of Brahman the one world soul, central to the entire complexus of created reality.

Hindu Prayer Life

Man himself is merely an individual expression of

the underlying reality of Brahman, the subtle essence, or hidden center of the universe. The totality of creation is conceived as having a single soul which animates every living part. Every living man, woman and child has a unique soul which is called Atman. Atman is the true self, the hidden self, but it too is more properly a particular expression of Brahman, and therefore though each man's Atman is distinct from every other Atman, it is nevertheless a part of the great Brahman.

The holy men of India teach that man must learn his true nature. Too often men identify themselves with the self they know. This surface self is just a passing reality. Those who fail to search for Atman, their innermost soul, fail to find the face of Brahman within them, and miss the real meaning of life. Yoga is an attempt to help man to find the supreme reality by finding their own life center.

The ultimate goal of life is the attainment of Nirvana, a state where man escapes from surface preoccupations and illusions, by reaching his Atman and thereby attaining union with his deepest God-self. Since all visible reality is held in low esteem, as merely a transitory, irrelevant phase of the life force, the religious Hindu tends to drift further and further away from what we call reality. He does this precisely because he chooses to deny that it is reality. The only reality is Brahman, the real one, the invisible world-soul.

Each life is lived and then it ends. If at the end of life we have discovered the secret and lived according to its law, we will reappear in a new existence with a higher degree of participation in the life of Brahman; this is the concept of reincarnation: The human soul, or Atman, must go somewhere, and it does. It is absorbed into Brahman, and will eventually emerge in a new day to take a new form. What that form will be depends entirely on how well, or how poorly the individual person gained awareness of his true self.

The law of Karma refers to this cycle of life: "A man reaps at that age, whether infancy, youth or old age, that which he had sowed in his previous birth. A man gets in life what he is fated to get, and even a god cannot make it otherwise" (Garuba Purana).

Nirvana means total absorption into the ground of being, where individuality is snuffed out and union with God is achieved perfectly, like a drop of water returning to the ocean. Until that state is attained, the Hindu believes he must wander through life, age after age, either in the form of an animal, an insect, a king or a beggar.

The discipline designed to help the Hindu achieve his goal in life is called Yoga.

Yoga is based on a theology which teaches two paths or levels of development in approaching God: the Path of Desire and the Path of Renunciation.

The Path of Desire begins with man's craving for pleasure. Hindu faith says go after it, it is good. But eventually the Path of Desire teaches that pleasure is essentially unsatisfying because it is too private, too restricting. It leaves one still hungry for more. The Path of Desire continues when one learns to leave pleasure as a goal and seek after worldly success. But worldly success is also unsatisfying; it is too competitive and precarious. Since it too centers on self, it is by nature limited, but worst of all it is only a temporary thing, it fades away.

Having lived through these experiences, man should then begin to see the wisdom of a better way: the Path of Renunciation. If the Path of Pleasure could satisfy, the Path of Renunciation would never be needed. But it is needed, and the Path of Renunciation begins with the ideal of service to others. In itself service is superior to all forms of self-interest, but it too is limited and transitory. The individual is limited in his ability to serve others. There is frustration and pain in this path; it lacks the reward of self-awareness. More is desired by man.

Beyond service, there is within the Path of Renunciation the ultimate Path of Liberation found in contemplation. By touching the infinite center of one's being, man transcends finitude; he contacts divine wisdom, overcomes ignorance, attains the fullness of life and achieves self-realization. Futility, boredom and frustration vanish, for union with Brahman is man's final goal. This is the purpose of Yoga, to lead men to liberation.

The Path of Liberation is explored in many ways, and the art of Yoga employs an amazing variety of techniques to attain it. There are four major categories in the practice of Yoga. Depending on the temperament of the person, he may choose to pursue union with Brahman either through contemplation, love, work or exercise.

1. Ynana Yoga is intellectual. It aims at self-realization through the use of the mind. It is essentially contemplative. Through knowledge and mental discipline, the yogi concentrates on Brahman, conceived as an impersonal world-soul, achieving a union so intense that he no longer feels his own body. To him pleasure and pain are one and the same. He no longer lives in this world. This path is reserved for the few.

2. Bhakiti Yoga is easier to follow. It is union through love. God is envisioned as personal and loving.

The yogi directs his love toward God. His goal is union with God himself; he acts for no other motive. God is imagined in various ways to educe this loving response. Some think of him as a protector, some as an intimate friend, some as a loving father, and some as a beloved spouse. The ultimate goal is very much like the Christian ideal of perfect charity, where all things are loved because God is loved, and God animates all things.

3. Karma Yoga is for the activist. Union with Brahman is attained through work. Rather than working for worldly success, they work for the glory of God. The Karmi acts as though each thing he does is the last thing he will ever do. The pursuit of perfection in daily work as a means of pleasing God is well-known in Catholic religious communities, but it was practiced in Hinduism centuries before Christ.

4. Hatha Yoga is most familiar in the West. It involves physical exercise of the body. The idea is to discipline the body in such a way as to bring it under total control, thus liberating the mind, freeing it from the distractions of joy and sorrow, pleasure and pain, peace and anxiety. In each case the Yogi seeks the union of Atman-Brahman, and when this is attained he has reached Nirvana.

There is no denying that Hinduism is characterized as an escapist religion. The emphasis is placed on a denial of life and flight from this world. However it would not be accurate to say that Hinduism is coextensive with the practice of Yoga. Yoga is only one aspect of Hindu prayer and religious dedication. To get the feeling of the rich variety of Hindu prayers and beliefs one must review the sacred writings which were briefly outlined in the beginning of this chapter.

The *Rig Veda* which means "the book of saving

knowledge," is the spiritual legacy of a group of barbarian tribesmen from Central Asia. There are more than a thousand psalms contained in it and the following one is addressed to Agni, the god of fire.

> May Agni, the presenter of oblations, the attainer of success in works, ever truthful, highly illustrious for many noble deeds, divine, come hither with the celestials.

> Whatever good, O Agni, thou mayest confer upon the giver of oblations that, indeed, O Angiras, belongs to thee.

> Bowing unto thee mentally, O Agni, we approach thee daily, both morning and evening.

> Thee, the radiant, the protector of sacrifices unobstructed by Rakahasas, the perpetual illuminator of truth and increasing in thine own room.

> Like unto a father to his son, O Agni, be easily accessible unto us; be ever present with us for our well-being.

The following hymn from another book of the *Rig Veda*, is ethereal in tone and reveals the same spirit we find in many other sacred writings. Do you see any phrases that remind you of the Jewish Bible?

> The gods have not ordained hunger to be our death, even to the well-fed man comes death in various shape.

> The riches of the generous man never waste away, while he who will not give finds none to comfort him.

> The man with food in store who, when the needy comes in miserable case begging for bread to eat,

> Hardens his heart against him—even when of old he did his service—finds not one to comfort him.

> Bounteous is he who gives unto the beggar who comes to him in want of food and feeble.

> Success attends him in the shout of battle. He makes a friend of him in future troubles.

> No friend is he who will offer nothing to his friend and comrade who comes imploring food

Let him depart—no home is that to rest in—and rather seek a stranger to support him.

Let the rich satisfy the poor implorer, and bend his eye upon a longer pathway.

Riches come now to one, now to another, and like the wheels of cars are ever rolling.

The hands are both alike; their labour differs. The yield of sister milchkine is unequal.

Twins even differ in their strength and vigour: two, even kinsmen, differ in their bounty.

The *Upanishads* are the interpretations and commentaries made of the obscure texts of the *Vedas*. The following sacred commentary is from the *Aitareya Upanishad*, and it explores the nature and destiny of the individual soul.

Verily from the beginning he (the Self) is in man as a germ, which is called seed.

This seed, which is strength gathered from all the limbs of the body, he (the man) bears as self in his self (body). When he commits the seed to the woman, then he (the father) causes it to be born. That is his first birth.

That seed becomes the self of the woman, as if one of her own limbs. Therefore it does not injure her.

She nourishes his (her husband's) self (the son) within her. She who nourishes is to be nourished.

The woman bears the germ. He (the father) elevates the child even before the birth, and immediately after.

When he thus elevates the child both before and after his birth, he really elevates his own self,

For the continuation of these worlds (men), for thus are these worlds continued.

This is his second birth.

He (the son), being his self, is then placed in his stead for the performance of all good works.

But his other self (the father) having done all he has to do, and having reached the full measure of his life, departs.

And departing from hence he is born again. That is his third birth . . .

Who is he whom we meditate on as Self? Which is the Self?

That by which we see form, that by which we hear sound, that by which we perceive smells, that by which we utter speech, that by which we distinguish sweet and not sweet, and what comes from the heart and the mind, namely, perception, command, understanding, knowledge, wisdom, seeing, holding, thinking, considering, readiness (or suffering), remembering, conceiving, willing, breathing, loving, desiring?

No, all these are various names only of knowledge (the true Self), consisting of knowledge, is Brahman . . . All the five elements, earth, air, ether, water, fire—these and those which are, as it were, small and mixed, and seeds of this kind, and that kind, born from eggs, born from the womb, born from heat, born from germs, horses, cows, men, elephants, and whatsoever breathes, whether walking or flying, and what is immovable—all that is produced by knowledge (the Self). Knowledge is its cause.

Knowledge is Brahman.

QUESTIONS TO THINK ABOUT

1. Hindus are more accepting of the religions of other people than are Christians, Jews, or Muslims. In your opinion is this good or bad? Or both? Explain.

2. How is Nirvana similar or dissimilar to the Christian concept of heaven?

3. The Hindu urge to de-emphasize this world in searching for one's innermost soul has been described by some as "escapist." Do you agree with this evaluation? Why or why not?

8
BUDDHISM

Generally speaking, Buddhism is to Hinduism what the Protestant Reformation was to Roman Catholicism. The Buddha was a Martin Luther preaching against certain elements of Hinduism. Today the two religions, having coexisted in India for nearly 2500 years, are like two threads woven into a single cloth. Hinduism, the all-pervasive religion of India, has absorbed Buddhism to a great extent, and both modes of thinking influence the practical life of the average Indian.

The Story of the Buddha

About 500 B.C. the Buddha, whose real name was Siddartha Gautama, was born in a wealthy family. His father was a chief, or raga, of the Sakya clan. It is said that in his childhood the young prince was spoiled with golden toys and silk clothing; servants tended to his every wish. He grew to manhood in a closed environment and knew very little of the world outside the palace grounds. One day he wandered outside the gates, and came in contact for the first time with the squalor and misery of the Indian people. He was an extremely sensitive young man, and the sight of such suffering sickened him. Depressed and discontented with his own superficial life, he began to reject everything—his riches, his title and the prospect of a comfortable future in the home of his father.

He was passionately alive with a desire to leave home and search out the meaning of his life. Trained in Brahmanism from his earliest years, Siddartha believed in reincarnation and the law of Karma, but these doctrines did not satisfy his thirst for wisdom. The glories of Hinduism left him still hungering for more. Naturally, his first instinct was to search more deeply within the rich traditions of his own religion. Prince Gautama was a newly married man with a young son when he decided to leave everything. He is said to have exclaimed one night when looking at his small child: "This is a new and strong tie which I have to break." He fled his home, renouncing all his wealth, and joined the Brahmins, the Hindu priestly caste. After long periods of fasting and mortification he found himself to be no wiser, and another heroic decision was made. He left the priesthood and went off again on his own.

After years of searching and near despair a great event took place in his life. One day, sitting beneath the Bo tree, which means "the tree of wisdom," contemplating life and its meaning, he became aware of an idea which he considered to be the central truth of human life: only by extinguishing all selfish desires can man ever hope to find happiness.

The name "Buddha" means "The Enlightened One" and it is the name Gautama took after his experience under the Bo tree. His fame spread rapidly as he preached his message to thousands of pilgrims who came to hear his revolutionary teachings. He challenged the Hindu structure of belief by rejecting fatalism. The Buddha taught that no one need be caught in the inevitable cycle of Karma; each person could learn to extricate himself from his suffering by conquering selfish desires.

The Buddha died about 480 B.C., after founding an order of monks. No one could actually replace him, so no successor was appointed. For nearly four centuries all his teachings were passed on in an oral tradition. Buddhism was seen as an esoteric sect at first; its doctrine was designed for the few who had the wisdom to follow the great teacher, and not for the masses. Nevertheless it reached the masses in time.

In this way, Buddhism remained just another minor sect of Hinduism until the third century, B.C., when a king named Asoka converted and made it the religion of his state. In its primitive form. Buddhism was called Hinayana; it then evolved and became known as Mahayana. Language always plays an important role in the development of religion.

Pali was the natural language of Buddha. King Asoka had the oral tradition of the Hinayana written in Pali. These books were eventually accepted by the Buddhists living in Ceylon, Burma and Siam. Another set of scripture, however, grew up in the Sanskrit language, and these bore the imprint of influences from other cultures in the Far East. These were called the Mahayana Canons. They were less negative and more worldly than the early Pali Canons, but the Sanskrit scriptures tended to make Buddha into a divine being, something he himself deplored in his own lifetime when followers revered him with excessive devotion. The evolution of Buddhism extends from these early developments before Christ right down to the 1970's. We shall consider Zen Buddhism in the following sections.

What Buddhists Believe

The Buddha reacted against the complexity and

fatalism of Hinduism. He rejected the cycle of reincarnation as a necessary way to self-realization. He chose a more direct path to Nirvana and taught his disciples that they could ascend the ladder of life through their own efforts without the intervention of the many gods of Hinduism. Buddha denied that there were outside agents helping or hindering man in his search for happiness. He also discarded the caste system. No one was born closer to Nirvana than anyone else; any man, woman or child could find his own happiness by escaping the complexities of Hinduism, and concentrating on the elimination of selfish desires.

Five hundred years before Christ, Siddartha Gautama, the Buddha, believed and taught that man created his own heaven and his own hell. The keystone to his religious teachings is called the Four Noble Truths.

1. Man's life is filled with misery and unhappiness. This everyone can plainly see.

2. But this misery and unhappiness is man's own doing; it has been caused by selfish desires.

3. Selfish desires can be eliminated completely, and therefore so can man's unhappiness.

4. There is an eightfold path that leads to the elimination of selfish desire.

> Ye that will tread the Middle-Road,
>   whose course
> Bright reason traces, and soft quiet
>   smooths,
> Ye who will take the high Nirvana-Way
>   list the four Noble Truths.

The Buddha wanted to help his followers take responsibility for their life and happiness, and not to sit idly waiting for a new life to correct the misery of this one. Suffering exists, and selfish craving is the direct cause of personal suffering. Renounce all selfish desires and be liberated. His way to freedom is expressed in a system, or technique of training, called the eightfold path, which is really nothing more than a form of morality. The eightfold path is a series of correct dispositions and actions which must be mastered. "It is right view (or understanding), right thought (or purpose), right speech, right conduct, right means of livelihood (or vocation), right effort, right alertness (or mind-control) and right meditation."

Each step depends on the completion of the former. The path is merely a means to the end, Nirvana; it is a stripping away of avarice, ambition, lust and all the other vices, in favor of selfless love. You will notice that Buddha does not concentrate on God or the worship of God. This is one reason why Eastern religions are often called "man-centered" rather than "God-centered." Nevertheless the goal of all this searching is Nirvana—union with the ultimate reality.

There have been many schools and sects within Buddhism, each striving to be a chastening simplification of the many possibilities within Hinduism. Buddha rejected the idea of an authoritative caste which had infused, or special knowledge. His teachings were intended for an elect few. His followers started with no authority structure, no infallibility, no traditions, no rituals, no superstitions, but every evolving body throughout history eventually divides and becomes more complicated with time. Nearly 1,000 years after Buddha died, a new reform took place. A Buddhist monk in China reacted against his particular training and began a new simplification of Buddhism. The monk's name was Bodhidharma, and Ch'an was the Chinese name of his system. In Japan it was called Zen.

Zen Buddhism

Zen is a technique, or method, by which a person can attain union with the ultimate one. It rejects all the elaborate discipline which the monks put into Buddhism through the centuries, and aims at the center of the target without elaborate ritual or preparation. The idea is simple enough. Since revelation, or inner illumination, comes not by tedious strivings but by a sudden spontaneous intuition, "like a light turning on," monastic traditions are useless.

Many rituals and regulations had grown around the simple teachings of Buddha. Bodhidharma began to teach his own system for attaining the final goal of life. His movement is anti-intellectual and anti-theoretical, striving once again for the purest, simplest path to God. To understand Zen, one must simply be exposed to a few of the *koans*, or riddles, which present insoluble problems for the purpose of shocking, or catapulting, the student into a new level of awareness. For instance, the master points to a flag waving in the breeze and asks his student, "What is moving, the flag or the wind?" Keep in mind there is no pat answer for any *koan*; the student must discover an answer for himself. The answer of the student might be, "Neither, for both are merely in the mind."

Another: "What is the Buddha?" The student answers, "Two-pounds of flax." It is a way of saying that the question itself is absurd, unanswerable; it is a way of remaining detached from the mystery while being immersed in it.

The Zen Buddhist is not on a trip from life; he wants above all to enter deeply into ordinary human existence; monasticism and all its mysterious traditions are cast aside. He believes he will find truth in ordinary life, all about him, and not in the esoteric experiences of mystic teachers. Each must discover truth within himself. The teacher merely guides one to the awakening.

"What is enlightenment?" asks the pupil. "Usual life is enlightenment," replies the master.

In meditation the follower of Zen takes a sitting position with legs crossed and the soles of the feet pointing up. The eyes are half-closed, the hands are in a receiving position at rest before him. The lotus seat position is the one attributed to Buddha when he was enlightened under the Bo tree. It is an attempt to go back to the purity of Buddha's own experience. The meditator empties himself of all thoughts, memories and imaginations.

The Zen master teaches the message of Zen. A student graduates after mastering about 50 *koan* problems. The *koans* excite an intense seeking for truth. For those interested in studying Zen it might be well to realize at the outset that a full course of training takes about 30 years.

The Practices of Modern Buddhism

Zen is basically a mystery, something which cannot be easily grasped or explained. It is a technique, or method, by which a person can attain union with the ultimate one. But the technique itself cannot be spelled out in words. Consequently, it can only be learned through training sessions with an experienced instructor who leads rather than informs or instructs. Zen must be discovered by means of an illumination of the mind.

You might find it helpful reading some of the sacred writings of Zen to get an idea of the direction of its philosophy. The following is from Zen Patriarch Yoka.

Since I found the path to truth
I am certain that one should not esteem
life or death.

Walking is Zen,
Sitting is also Zen.

If I speak I am silent,
If I rest I hasten:

In essence everything is
The immovable, original one.

If I am threatened by spear and sword,
I never blink an eyelash.

If poison sneaks toward me,
I am not afraid.

How often have I been reborn,
How often did I die again!

Incessant and immeasurable
Life and death lasted.

Yet since I, like a flash of lightning,
Experience the highest truth
I care no more about good or bad fortune.

The oldest Zen poem conveys a similar spirit of peaceful resignation to all experience, taking each thing as it comes, without fuss, without distress.

The perfect way is without difficulty.
Save that it avoids picking and choosing
Only when you stop liking and disliking
Will all be clearly understood.
A split hair's difference,
And heaven and earth are set apart!
If you want to get the plain truth,
Be not concerned with right and wrong.
The conflict between right and wrong
Is the sickness of the mind.

Another short Zenrin poem appropriate for the season:

> Sitting quietly, doing nothing,
> Spring comes and the grass
> grows by itself.

Finally, a poem that sums up life as simply as could ever be done:

> We eat, sleep and get up;
> This is our world;
> All we have to do after that
> Is to die.

Actually, Zen is a course of self-enlightenment which is independent of written texts. The above poems are merely outpourings of Zen philosophers who have acquired the right spirit. Enlightenment is not transferred through reading, but rather through the sudden flash of illumination which comes from the realization of a new truth. A Zen student might sit for days with legs crossed, the soles of his feet and his hands open before him. He empties himself of all sense experience, opening himself to what Westerners might call "mystical illumination." He knows that God communicates with man in ways other than through sense experience. It is the Buddhist way of prayer: to be still and listen to the movement of God within the depths of his own being, and to search.

The discipline and zeal with which the Buddhist pursues his goal of union with God is most admirable. We can all learn something from the dedication of the devout Buddhist.

QUESTIONS TO THINK ABOUT

1. How was the "conversion" of Prince Gautama like or unlike that of Abraham, Mohammed, or perhaps Paul? What makes a person become converted?

2. What are "selfish desires"? Can you list them? Is it possible to eliminate them? If so, what is left when all "selfish desires" are gone?

3. What is the connection between physical position and prayer? What is the value of the lotus position for the Buddhist, prostration for the Muslim, kneeling for the Christian?

9
THE RELIGIONS OF THE FAR EAST: CHINA AND JAPAN

China's Heritage

China is much in the news lately but hardly a word is mentioned about her three principal religions: Confucianism, Taoism and Buddhism. Since Buddhism was treated in the preceding chapter, we will concentrate here on China's more ancient religious heritage, Confucianism and Taoism. Maoist China is still so obscure to Westerners that it is difficult for us to assess the present condition of the ancient Chinese religious culture. The so-called "unchanging East" is still in the throes of turmoil. The calm surface of China a few years back broke into volcanic disruption with the fanatical activity of the Red Guard. Future tremors of shocking magnitude might still be in store for China; we do not know. Yet we do know this: the Old China cannot have been erased in one stroke. While it is true that China will never again be the same after the Maoist impact, the archaic orthodoxy of Confucianism, Taoism and Buddhism still represents a religious heritage of 25 centuries. This cannot be ripped from the conscious and subconscious lives of more than 600 million people in a few decades. In fact, ancient China provided a good basis for the new China.

Like communism, these three religions are more

concerned with man's well-being than with religious worship, as such. In spite of the many differences found in China's traditions, it is characteristic for the Chinese to harmonize opposites, making them compatible and complementary. In past centuries the majority of the Chinese people were comfortable taking bits and pieces from each tradition, molding their own personal religious life as it suited them. All of this was interlaced with primitive forms of worship.

The earliest religious beliefs of China were animistic. The sun and moon, the trees and winds, the birds and animals, for centuries all were venerated as possessing spirits. Ancestor-worship grew out of this mentality, for spirits live on even after death. This reverence for deceased ancestors explains much of the emphasis in the teachings of Confucious on respect for elders.

For centuries the Chinese were ruled by emperors who were seen as high priests invested by the gods with extraordinary powers. This may explain the phenomenal exaltation of Mao Tse-tung. The Chinese, like the Egyptians, have tended to divinize their monarchs.

Monotheism began in the Shang Dynasty (1700 to 1100 B.C.) when a belief developed in a supreme being called Shang-Ti. However this did not mean that the traditional polytheistic gods were rejected. The emperors simply focused greater emphasis on Shang-Ti as supreme. Later, with the Chou Dynasty, a shift took place and more reverence was paid to an impersonal god called Tien. The Chou emperors then avoided any reference to Shang-Ti. The emperors of subsequent dynasties became the high priests of Tien with exclusive right to offer sacrifices to heaven. The great Altar of Heaven was built at Peking during the Ming Dynasty (17th Century A.D.) and imperial sacrifices to the gods continued in the forbidden city until the birth of the Republic of China in 1911.

Prior to this the country was one huge feudal system. The emperor alone worshiped the highest God; the princes were responsible for venerating lesser cosmic deities, the feudal lords and governors prayed to minor spirits. All of these gods supported all the injustices of the feudal system. The rejection of divine worship in China today is not at all unrelated to the rejection of a corrupt feudal system.

Confucianism

In 551 B.C., before Socrates was to pioneer an era of philosophical inquiry in ancient Greece, and about the same time that Prince Guatama (the Buddha) began his reform of Hinduism in India, Confucius was born in the Province of Shantung, China. His father, Kung Shu-Liang Ho, a 70-year-old member of the lesser nobility, married a fifteen-year-old girl; their only child was called Kung-Fu-Tzu, or "Kung the Teacher," leading to the Latinized version of his name: Confucius.

To understand Kung's writings one must appreciate the situation in which he lived. In 500 B.C. China was in turmoil. The Chou Dynasty was all but finished and domestic wars were raging as feudal lords drove their armies to butcher one another. Thousands of lives were ruthlessly taken in this futile violence. The desire for law and order is never so strong as in a state of chaos. Out of the rubble China's first absolute emperor was to emerge, but the price of this new rule was heavy. Many of the landed gentry, nobles, artists, and intellectuals were thrown out of favor and out of power.

Confucius was one of the displaced persons. He was not a wealthy man, but he was an intellectual who found himself without recognition or position. He wanted a secure and peaceful society. He had begun serious study around the age of fifteen and became an expert in Chinese history and tradition by his early twenties. He loved tradition. He was a conservative; respectful of authority and nostalgic for the idealized, purified forms of the past. In fact his whole ethical system, which he believed God sent him to teach, was basically a revival of feudalism in a stricter, nobler and more purified form.

Although he began working as a low-level civil servant, Confucius felt a strong desire to become a teacher, and so he did, for many years. But at the age of fifty he entered government to become the mayor of a city. From that position he was elevated to Minister of Justice in the principality of Lu. His success was phenomenal in that he brought about a change of manners in the people. The men of Lu acted with honesty, the women were chaste and obedient. As Confucius grew in wisdom, his fame spread, attracting many students all over China. His standards were always high, so he accepted only an elite group of intellectually ambitious disciples. "To him who has no enthusiasm I shall not open up the truth." He believed that wise men should bring their wisdom to the marketplace for the instruction of rulers and for the ultimate good of society. He was never recognized as he had hoped. "No intelligent ruler arises to take me as his master . . . my time has come to die." He died in the year 479 B.C., leaving behind a legacy of writings that have influenced Chinese thinking for more than 2000 years. But his message was not immediately accepted.

Around 255 B.C., China was united for the first time under the Chin Dynasty. The new aristocracy accused the scholars of Confucianism of being reactionary, disciples of the past who were out to discredit the new order. This was a period of great persecution; the thinking of Confucianism was banned and nearly 500 scholars were put to death. During this period Taoism began to grow in influence, but time changes everything. By 141 B.C., the new Han Dynasty lifted the ban and Emperor Wu Ti established Confucianism as a state cult. Later it developed into a religion with priests, temples and ceremonies. Sacrifices were offered at the tomb of Confucius and thereafter emperors competed with their predecessors in honoring the famous philosopher.

The Faith of Confucianism

Confucius did not claim to found a new religion; his teachings are primarily ethical. He was never revered by his early followers as anything but their "Foremost Teacher." His teaching was simply a system of ethics super-added to the existing religious culture of his times. There was already in his time faith in the supreme deity, Tien. Confucius accepted this tradition and encouraged the worship of Tien, the supreme ruler of the universe, who is often referred to in his writings as "Heaven." "Heaven is the only Great One." "I have heard that life and death are allotted, that wealth and honors are in Heaven's hand . . . from Him the wise man receives his wisdom, the good man his virtue."

In the *Aphorisms of Confucius* under the heading "The Emotional and Artistic Life of Confucius," we read,

What Confucius took very seriously were: The ceremonial bath before religious worship, war and sickness.

Someone asked Confucius about the meaning of the Grand Sacrifice to the Imperial Ancestors, and Confucius said: "I don't know. One who knows the meaning of the Grand Sacrifice would be able to rule the world as easily as pointing a finger at the palm."

When Confucius offered sacrifice to his ancestors, he felt as if his ancestors were present bodily, and when he offered sacrifice to the other gods, he felt as if the gods were present bodily. Confucius said, "If I don't offer sacrifice by being personally present, it is as if I didn't sacrifice at all."

Mangum Chia asked, "Why do people say that it is better to get on good terms with the kitchen god than with the god of the southwestern corner of the house?" Confucius replied, "Nonsense, if you have committed sins against Heaven, you haven't got a god to pray to."

Rsekung wanted to do away with the ceremony of sacrificing the lamb in winter. Confucius said, "Ah Sze, you love the lamb, but I love the institution."

Confucius said, "Respect the heavenly and earthly spirits and keep them at a distance."

It is often said that Confucius had little interest in God, and to some extent this is true, but only partially true. While Confucius was not primarily concerned with religion in his writings, obviously he was a religious man. He was also interested in improving society, in rebuilding the moral climate of civilization; this was the purpose of his writing. Religion was the substructure of his whole philosophy.

The core of his ethical system is expressed in Chinese by the word *li*, which basically means law and order. Confucius says: "The principles of *li* and righteousness serve as the principles of social discipline. By means of these principles people try to maintain the official status of rulers and subjects, to teach the parents and children and elder brothers and younger brothers and husbands and wives to live in harmony, to establish social institutions. . . . Through this principle of rational social order (*li*) everything becomes right in the family, the state and the world."

He idealized the notion of the correct man, or the gentleman, and every act of every person was weighed against what might be expected of the gentleman. Confucius set about to explain how man should act in all his private, family and public relationships. The afterlife was not his concern. "Till we know about the living, how are we to know about the dead?" He concentrated on the immediate relationship of the family.

"It is not possible for a man to teach others who cannot teach his own family, for from loving examples of one family, the whole of society becomes loving; while from the ambition and perverseness of one man, the whole state may be led to rebellion and disorders. Such is the nature of influence."

Two great teachers of Confucianism succeeded the Master in later years: Meng K'o (known to Westerners as Mencius) and Hsun Tzu. Both men believed firmly in the need for education and social formation but they took different approaches to the problem.

Mencius believed that man was basically good in spirit. He attributed the presence of evil to ignorance and claimed that ignorance came about because of a lack of proper training and example. He upheld the importance of maintaining a childlike spirit because the child is naturally good. Hsun Tzu disagreed with him. He claimed that man was naturally evil, children included, and that it was (*li*) training and discipline which overcomes evil.

Chu Hsi, the Thomas Aquinas of Confucianism,

did not appear until 1130 to 1200 A.D. In his system of thought he worked to synthesize the best of Buddhism and Taoism into Confucianism.

All three men took pains to purge Confucianism of all religious elements. Confucius says: "Let us leave the heavens to the angels and the sparrows." Right order here and now is the theme.

In his book, "My Country and My People," Lin Yutang, the famous Chinese philosopher, wrote the following description of the spirit of Chinese people, a spirit which was captured and transmitted by the teachings of Confucius:

> For the Chinese the end of life lies neither in life after death, for the idea that we live in order to die, as taught by Christianity, is incomprehensible; nor in the satisfaction of accomplishment, for that is too vainglorious; nor yet in progress for progress sake, for that is meaningless. The true end, the Chinese have decided in a singularly clear manner, lies in the enjoyment of a simple life, especially the family life, and in harmonious social relationships. There is no doubt that the Chinese are in love with life, which is so sad and yet so beautiful, and in which moments of happiness are so precious because they are so transient.

Confucius was a traditionalist. He prided himself not as a creator of new thought, but as a transmitter of ancient Chinese treasures. His great writings are basically a synthesis of the classics of the Chou period (1100 B.C. - 481 B.C.). There are six great works attributed to him:

1. *The Book of Changes* (Yi-Ching)—expounds the yang-yin theory. His main thesis concerns the ever-changing circumstances of life, advocating the need for harmony and balance between yin and yang. It calls for a submission of self to the objective requirements of right order.

2. *The Book of History* (Shu-Ching)—is the story of the great kings of ancient China.

3. *The Book of Odes* (Shu-Ching)—contains the songs and ballads of his times.

4. *The Book of Events* (Ch'un Ch'iu)—contains biographical material on the lives of the rulers of his home Province of Lu.

5. *The Book of Rites* (Li Chi)—contains a listing of ceremonies with commentary upon them.

6. *The Analects*—is a collection of poems and sayings of the Confucius Master. This is his best known book. Before Mao's little red book this was the gospel of China.

Remember those sayings? Confucius says: If you make a mistake, admit it and mend your ways. Confucius says: A gentleman sees a question from all sides, without bias. Confucius says: Goodness is three-sided: in private it is courtesy, in public it is diligence, in relationships, it is loyalty. Confucius says: Never do to others what you would not like them to do to you. Basically the Master was trying to instill the old feudal code of rites and etiquette into a universal system of ethics for a new age.

For Confucius, morality is not observed out of obedience to divine commands, but rather out of an innate sense of right order. Though the Master thought of himself as one chosen by heaven to teach this correct way of life, he never alluded to any of his precepts as God's will. Right reason, and the eternal pursuit of order, harmony and balance are the sole basis of his appeal and his authority. Confucianism, strictly speaking, is not a religion at all—it is an ethical system, developed by a social scientist who worshiped his god privately.

Taoism and Yang-Yin

Like the West, China has had a long legacy of myth, legend, rituals, and magic. It has gone through centuries of religious evolution. But unlike the West it has tended to organize the whole heritage not around the concept of a single god but around the concept of man. The interplay of forces in human life must be managed and controlled. This is the art of living.

The Chinese spirit must be analyzed in the light of yang-yin if one is to understand the significance of the past or the shape of the future. This ancient formula of wisdom dates as far back as 1000 B.C., and has deeply penetrated the Chinese view of reality. The power of yang-yin has enabled the Chinese people to ride the waves of history with detachment and dignity.

Yang-yin might be called the fundamental outlook of the Chinese. This outlook underlies all beliefs and traditions, past and present. Yang-yin means that all of life is an eternal interplay between opposing forces: activity and receptivity; male and female; sound and silence; light and darkness; matter and form. Activity and receptivity (yang-yin) are signs of interaction which give birth to everything that is. Male is completed by female (yang-yin); sound is completed by hearing (yang-yin); light has no meaning apart from darkness (yang-yin); water has no form without a container (yang-yin). All of these opposites coexist and pursue one another in search of harmony and resolution.

You've probably seen the symbol of yang-yin many times. It is a circle divided by a curved line; one-half is all white with a black spot, the other half is all black with a white spot. The meaning of this symbol is both beautiful and profound. The circle expresses the limits of human life. There is opposition within the circle, but harmony is attained without conflict. There is the tension of opposition within the circle, but order exists, balance and harmony are possible. This in effect is the goal of life. Too much Confucianism is no good; too much Taoism is no good; a little of each is better.

The art of living is expressed in the effort to harmonize opposites (yang and yin) into manageable balance.

This leads to a discussion of Taoism, for Taoism and Confucianism are deeply related in the Chinese religious experience.

The natural counterbalance to Confucianism was found in Taoism, the second religion of China. The old master Lao Tze (604 B.C. to 524 B.C.) also reacted against the lawlessness and moral chaos of his day, but unlike his younger contemporary Confucius, Lao was a mystic, not a practical reformer. His teaching was more spiritual than ethical, a teaching not unlike the wisdom of Buddha.

The name "Taoism" (pronounced "dowism") comes from the Chinese word Tao, meaning "path" or "way." The closest thing in modern jargon to the meaning of Taoism, is in the title of the song, "Let It Be." The belief of Tao implies an approach to life which is natural, i.e., in harmony with the rest of the universe. A respect for one's own nature, and the nature of things as they are, leads us to the realization that we must pace ourselves in life; we must bend in circumstances in order to survive. Too much haste leads to exhaustion before the task is completed, or worse, causes failure due to poor planning. A sculptor must not strike the stone arbitrarily against the grain, or he will destroy the entire work. The inner nature of things must be studied and respected.

The Faith of the Taoist

Modern Americans are conditioned to interpret a headache as a signal to take an aspirin; for the Taoist it is a sign that he must slow down and let go. The legendary founder of Taoism, Lao-Tze (the Grand Old Teacher), set down the basic principle of Tao, *wu wei* which means "let go," "let it happen." It is not a mental health program, but rather a way of life that reaches right up to the ordering of society, in regard to politics, the gospel of Tao, entitled *Tao Te Ching*, which means "The Way and Its Power," states:

> A leader is best
> When people barely know that
> he exists.
> . . . Of a good leader, who talks
> little,
> When his work is done, his aim
> fulfilled,
> They will all say, "We did this
> ourselves."

The philosophy of Tao existed in China a short while before Confucius (c. 500 B.C.) but it eventually became a religion which survived down through the centuries as a counterbalance to Confucius' heavily legalistic, rule-oriented ethical system. Taoism and Confucianism are like yang-yin, both complement one another. Yin is female—soft and bending (Taoism); yang is male—rigid and rational (Confucianism). The fusion of both has found its way into the Chinese mentality and culture.

Taoism has two forms. One contains elements of sorcery and superstition such as one finds in all primitive religions. The other is a rather esoteric form of mysticism only for an elect few. Each of these are based on the philosophy of intuitive respect for the "natural way life works itself out." It was all started by a wise sage who outlined a philosophy for sensible living, but by the second century A.D., Lao-Tze was worshiped by many as a chief god. Temples and a priesthood developed around his cult. In China today most Taoist temples are in disuse and the priestly caste is all but extinct.

The gospel of Taoism is a small book of about eighty-one chapters. It is filled with uplifting and inspiring wisdom urging man to empty himself of mundane desires. Much like Buddhism, it points the way to happiness through self-denial. The desires of man are extinguished and a state of quiet contentment emerges. This is Taoism, the way. Does it resemble anything you might have seen before?

Qualities of the Taoist

When the highest type of men hear the Tao (truth),
They practice it diligently.

When the mediocre type hear the Tao,
They seem to be aware yet unaware of it.

When the lowest type hear the Tao,
They break into loud laughter—

If it were not laughed at, it would not be Tao.

Therefore there is the established saying:
"Who understands Tao seems dull of comprehension,
Who is advanced in Tao seems to slip backwards;
Who moves on the even Tao (Path) seems to go up and
    down."

Superior virtue appears like a hollow (valley);
Sheer white appears like tarnished;

Great character appears like insufficient;
Solid character appears like infirm;
Pure worth appears contaminated.

Great space has no corners;
Great talent takes long to mature;
Great music is faintly heard;
Great Form has no contour;
And Tao is hidden without a name.

It is this Tao that is adept at lending (its power)
and bringing fulfillment.

Calm Quietude

The highest perfection is like imperfection,
And its use is never impaired.

The greatest abundance seems meagre,
And its use will never fail.

What is most straight appears devious;
The greatest cleverness appears like stupidity;
The greatest eloquence seems like stuttering,

Movement overcomes cold,
(But) keeping still overcomes heat.

Who is calm and quiet becomes the guide for the universe.

The People's Hearts

The Sage has no decided opinions and feelings,
But regards the people's opinions and feelings as his
own.

The good ones I declare good;
The bad ones I also declare good.
That is the goodness of virtue.

The Sage dwells in the world peacefully,
harmoniously,
The people of the world are brought into
a community of heart,
And the Sage regards them all as his own children.

Although Confucianism and Taoism went through
centuries of conflict between their scholars, the two systems merged in the course of time.

The Prayer Life of China

Ancestor worship is the true asceticism of the Chinese, whether they be Buddhists, Confucians or Taoists, or any combination thereof. The Chinese have an unusually strong sense of family solidarity extending beyond the grave to include deceased ancestors. For centuries most homes have had little shrines with mementos of the families' forefathers who are honored much in the same way that saints are venerated in Catholicism.

The families themselves are clustered in clans and a strong loyalty exists between them. A clan usually builds its own ancestral shrine for all clan members with the same name. These shrines compete with one another in splendor. They contain scrolls of the names of ancient ancestors; and ceremonies are conducted when a new member has died and is added to the scrolls.

Festivals and feasts are celebrated in and around the clan shrines, and special prayers on these occasions are offered seeking the help and protection of deceased loved ones.

Confucius did not devote himself to any study of heaven, but he knew religious feeling helped to stabilize family unity and he was in favor of any influence which supported the family, the basic unit of the social structure.

In the days of the feudal system, feudal lords were expected to offer a particular form of worship to the spirits of the hills and streams. If someone of lesser nobility offered such a sacrifice it was believed the gods would be offended. For centuries, a definite graded system of ritual and worship existed, and it was served by the priestly castes of varying degrees of dignity. The ritual worship of the Chinese has always been family oriented.

Today things are different. Maoist China is atheistic. The spirits of ancestors as objects of worship is debunked. Mao Tze-tung once said: "I hated Confucianism from the age of eight." Shrines are falling more and more into disuse. Foreign religions are scorned, and barely tolerated only as long as they serve the goals of the communist state. The Red Guard revolution in the 60's included a violent reaction against the practice of honoring elders. Newspapers printed pictures of old men and women having their heads shaved in public by Red Guard teenage mobs. This humiliation served to demonstrate the new freedom in China from ancient traditions. A far cry from Confucianism.

The old ways however do not die so easily. The passion of a movement tends to wane and the character of a people tends to remain constant. Yang-yin is the spirit of China. Even harsh regimentation and cold uniformity can hold sway for only as long as the people decide to tolerate it. A balance will be achieved, the pendulum will swing back, such is the Chinese spirit, such is the law of yang-yin.

Strangely enough the West has its own yang-yin. The cold war thaw has begun. The inevitability of coexistence with the communist block, and the impossibility of the "containment" philosophy of United States foreign policy, has brought about a complete change in East-West relations. Even the Church of Rome has changed, vis-à-vis communism. On April 18, 1973, the Vatican made a public overture for a "dialogue with Peking on the basis of Roman Catholic recognition that the thoughts of Chairman Mao Tse-tung also reflected

Christian values." The Sacred Congregation for the Evangelization of the Peoples, the Vatican's missionary department, issued the statement that Maoist doctrine "contains some directives that are in keeping with the great moral principles of the millenary Chinese civilization and find authentic and complete expression in modern social Christian teaching."

This is a major breakthrough in view of the past experience of relations between China and the Vatican, but the truth of it has always been present. Those who now search for common ground find a rich field in the wisdom of Mao. Whatever the means chosen to attain a goal might be, the goal itself may be seen as just and upright in many of its aspects. These new developments in world relations will hopefully lead to an era of less tension and more harmony. Even China would have to accept the inevitability of a changing tide. The ebb and flow of life is merely another aspect of yang-yin.

Japan's Heritage: Shintoism

Although Buddhism is found in Japan, the national religion of Japan is Shinto. There are over 95 million Japanese people, and it is estimated that 70 million of these are adherents of Shinto. There is a vast and complicated history to this religion intimately tied into the political history of Japan.

It was traditionally held that two gods created the world and gave birth to a sun goddess who is the ancestor of the mikado, or emperor. The divinity of the emperor was once the heart of the national character of Japan. In the 18th century there was a religious purging in which foreign elements such as Buddhism and Con-

fucianism were expelled. Shinto was declared the only
true religion and faith in the emperor's divine descent
was reinforced.

In 1867 Shinto became the religion of the state and
was placed under the jurisdiction of the Department of
the Interior. As such the religion became an instrument
of promoting patriotism and national loyalty. Other
religions were tolerated but in all cases the supreme authority of the state had to be acknowledged. The state
shrines dedicated to the worship of twelve emperors had
to be visited.

In 1946, after World War II, the Emperor of
Japan subservient to the Allied military rule, renounced
the myth of his divinity. Shinto was then disestablished
as the state religion. Among many of the Japanese, the
loss of the war was regarded as the defeat of the Shinto
gods.

Many changes have taken place since then. A wide
plurality of Shinto sects has emerged, many of them
fashioned after Western sects. Monotheism has been
proclaimed and the polytheism of Shinto rejected.
Today all kinds of religious experience can be found
under the Shinto umbrella, from sensitivity groups to
faith healers. Since the state no longer controls religion
the people are free to follow any bent they choose.

The Shinto religion has an organized priesthood
which is hereditary. Religious aspirations mainly of
gratitude and love are ritualized in celebrations of joy.
The shrines are usually small, not like Christian
churches. They are dwellings of the gods, not assembly
halls. Over 100,000 such dwellings, or shrines, still exist
in Japan.

A worshiper approaches the entrance through a
wooden gateway made of two posts topped by a slightly

curved crossbeam which projects on each side, a familiar sight in tourist books. Public rituals are conducted at fixed times. The gods are appeased, spirits are calmed and good will is invoked. The primitive roots of fear and superstition are very evident; however, there are no moral precepts, no commandments. Worship and morality are two distinct things.

Shinto is a subdued religion which makes very few demands of its adherents. Immorality is looked upon as simply the natural state of things. There is an awakening of the female liberation movement which is beginning to have a powerful upsetting effect on the national life of Japan. Until recently Japan has been exclusively a man's world. Women are beginning to catch on to the meaning of human rights and female dignity. In brief, modern Japan is rapidly becoming Westernized, economically, politically, intellectually and emotionally. Nevertheless, the predominant religion of the West, Christianity, still accounts for less than one percent of the population.

QUESTIONS TO THINK ABOUT

1. Is the Confucian more interested in behavior or worship? What about the Shintoist? The Muslim? The Christian? Do you believe there is a necessary connection between religion and morality?

2. Can you point to some examples of yang and yin in American society? In your own life? Give examples.

3. Is it possible for you, when faced with a problem, to face it simply by "letting go" as the Taoist would? Why or why not?

INDEX